Kerstin Söderblom

Queer-Affirming
Pastoral Care

VANDENHOECK & RUPRECHT

Bibliographic information published by the Deutsche Nationalbibliothek:
The Deutsche Nationalbibliothek lists this publication in the Deutsche
Nationalbibliografie; detailed bibliographic data available online: https://dnb.de.

© 2024 Vandenhoeck & Ruprecht, Robert-Bosch-Breite 10, D-37079 Göttingen,
an imprint of the Brill-Group
(Koninklijke Brill NV, Leiden, Netherlands; Brill USA Inc., Boston MA, USA;
Brill Asia Pte Ltd, Singapore; Brill Deutschland GmbH, Paderborn, Germany;
Brill Österreich GmbH, Vienna, Austria)
Koninklijke Brill NV includes the imprints Brill, Brill Nijhoff, Brill Schöningh,
Brill Fink, Brill mentis, Brill Wageningen Academic, Vandenhoeck & Ruprecht,
Böhlau and V&R unipress.

All rights reserved. No part of this work may be reproduced or utilized in any form
or by any means, electronic or mechanical, including photocopying, recording,or any
information storage and retrieval system, without prior written permission from
the publisher.

The original edition *Queersensible Seelsorge* was published in 2023.

Cover image: © rkit/Pixabay

Translation: Max Helmich
Proofreading: Dr. Carol Joyner
Typesetting: SchwabScantechnik, Göttingen
Printed and bound: CPI books, Leck
Printed in the EU

Vandenhoeck & Ruprecht Verlage | www.vandenhoeck-ruprecht-verlage.com

ISBN 978-3-525-60460-1

FOREWORD TO THE ENGLISH EDITION

"Could there not be an English translation of your book?" I was often asked by various European friends from the European Forum of LGBTI+ Christian Groups. *"But the book is about my experiences as a queer-affirming pastor and university chaplain in Germany",* I used to answer. Hence, I wrote about the specific religiopolitical context of the Protestant Church in Germany (EKD). Discussing the matter with several colleagues, I decided to have my book translated anyway. Aside from the religiopolitical settings, the concrete case studies and my evaluation of them present some general findings and insights: no matter how progressive church laws are, queer people of faith often have to struggle with certain challenges and obstacles in their home parishes or faith communities. Controversies around biblical hermeneutics and theological topics concerning diverse sexual orientations and gender identities are some of the biggest problems they have to face. Therefore, queer-affirming pastoral care is not an easy thing to do, anywhere in the world. What has to be taken into consideration? What can be said about biblical "clobber passages" that condemn homosexuality? What is a queer re-reading of biblical texts? What should be offered, to make pastoral care a queer-affirming endeavor? My book provides insights and suggestions that are valid not only for the individual case study in question, but also for general discernment. I hope that my book can encourage pastoral care givers in different countries to contextualize and adapt the material and develop queer-affirming pastoral care education and training in their specific countries and religious settings.

Kerstin Söderblom

FOREWORD

For more than twenty years, I have been working in various church positions as an openly lesbian pastor. Even as a young theology student, the human resources department of my church, the Protestant Church in Hesse and Nassau (EKHN), encouraged me not to give up my studies after coming out, stressing that they hired their staff based on their qualifications and not their lifestyles. Nevertheless, they also explained that my lifestyle could be an obstacle for some local church members. As it turned out, they weren't wrong; what lay ahead was a learning curve that would not always prove easy for all parties involved.

A lot has happened since I came out in the 1980s. Many regional churches in Germany now offer weddings or services of blessing for same sex couples. Most of them allow lesbian and gay pastors to live as couples in the parsonage and for trans* people to remain in their church jobs, even post transition.

However, if one looks at the worldwide ecumenical church landscape, churches are far too often part of the problem rather than part of the solution. Right-wing evangelicals of all denominations – also including non-religious fundamentalists and those taking extreme right-wing positions – are organizing internationally to stand up for traditional family values.

Quite a few pastors and church employees publicly condemn queer people in sermons and speeches, threatening them with hell and damnation. Some even incite their parishioners to hatred and exclusion, with Bible in hand. Again and again, queer people are excluded from congregations or religious groups after a voluntary or forced coming out. Social contacts and networks are lost in the process and it is not uncommon for queer people to be verbally or physically attacked. Cyril I, the Patriarch of the Russian Orthodox Church in Moscow, stated one reason for Russia's war of aggression against Ukraine was the need to protect Russian family values from the Western "gay epidemic" and Pride Parades.

Little wonder then, that queer-affirming pastoral care is still urgently needed today. Queer believers need safe spaces where they can talk about their experiences without having to justify them or fearing re-traumatization. They need places where they can experience that being queer and being a believer are not mutually exclusive, but in fact go together well.

This is exactly what I am passionate about as a pastor. I am committed to respect and equality for queer people in various places in the church – in preaching, in church discussion events, in educational work, in pastoral care, and in counseling. And right from the start, queer believers, or those in search of a religious home, have approached me for pastoral care and counseling. The need was and still is great. And yet, explicitly queer-friendly pastoral support is still hard to find in church circles.

The importance of queer-affirming pastoral care is also evident in my current work as a university pastor at the Evangelische Studierendengemeinde/ESG (Protestant University Chaplaincy) in Mainz, Germany. From the very beginning, students from very different disciplines have approached me about queer-affirming pastoral care and counseling. After all, young people too experience how difficult it is to be queer and religious on a daily basis. Fortunately, queer-affirming pastoral care services are well established in the Catholic (KHG) and Protestant university communities in Mainz. However, this is by no means the case everywhere.

Moreover, to my knowledge there has not been a single book published on this topic in the German-speaking world. Queer-affirming approaches are neither official topics in pastoral care training, nor in further and continuing education. And there is a long way to go, until they become concepts within the curriculum.

For all of these reasons, I decided at the beginning of 2022 to write down and evaluate my pastoral care experiences on these topics in the format of condensed case studies. A three-month study leave, which my regional church allows its pastors every ten years, gave me time and space to put the plan into action.

With this book, I hope to make queer-affirming pastoral care perspectives more comprehensible and deepen existing insights.

My wish is that it offers suggestions to those providing pastoral care today, as well as material for modules on queer-affirming pastoral care education and training.

Kerstin Söderblom

TABLE OF CONTENTS

FOREWORD TO THE ENGLISH EDITION 5
FOREWORD 7
INTRODUCTION 13

CLASSIFICATION 15

I   **What is pastoral care?** 15
    1 Approaching pastoral care 15
    2 My personal position 18
    3 Biblical-theological basic assumptions 19
    4 Approaching queer-theological research 24

PERCEPTION 27

II   **Context** 27
    1 "Outside the box" 27
    2 Learning paths 27
    3 #OutInChurch 28
    4 Pluralization of sexual orientations, life forms and gender identities 29
    5 Role models for self-acceptance 30
    6 Respectful pastoral care as an initial spark for commitment 31

III   **Case studies** 31
    1 Case study: "I don't know how to say it!" 32
        1.1 Meeting 32
        1.2 Queer re-reading of the Easter story 34
        1.3 Resonances 35
    2 Case Study: "I separate to find myself again!" 36
        2.1 Meeting 36
        2.2 Queer re-reading of the story of Jacob 38
        2.3 Resonances 40

	3	Case study: "It's hell!"	41
		3.1	Meeting	41
		3.2	Queer re-reading of the story of the prophet Elijah	43
		3.3	Resonances	46
	4	Case study: "I don't fit into any pigeonhole!"	46
		4.1	Meeting	46
		4.2	Queer re-reading of Joseph's story	48
		4.3	Resonances	50
	5	Case study: "What is normal, actually?"	51
		5.1	Meeting	51
		5.2	Queer re-reading of the double commandment of love	54
		5.3	Resonances	56

UNDERSTANDING 57

IV	First findings	57
	1 Framework: Safe places and reliable time frames	57
	2 Attitude: Appreciation and respect	57
	3 Knowledge: Knowing about minority stress	58
	4 Evaluation: Change of perspective and expansion of action	60
	5 Challenge: "Clobber Passages"	61
	6 Workshop: Queer re-readings of Biblical texts	62
	7 Reflection: The role of pastoral caregivers	62
V	Dealing with "Clobber Passages"	64
	1 Challenge	64
	2 Theological Classification and Explanation of the Clobber Passages	65
	3 Conclusion	71

IMPLEMENTATION 73

VI	Queer-affirming pastoral care in the context of ceremonial services	73
	1	Wedding and blessing services	73
		1.1	Request	74
		1.2	Queer re-reading of the Book of Ruth	75
		1.3	Resonances	78
		1.4	Conclusion	80
	2	Rainbow family baptism	81
		2.1	Request	81
		2.2	Queer re-reading of Isaiah 43:1b	82
		2.3	Resonances	82
		2.4	Conclusion	83

      3 Coming out in the confirmation group 84
          3.1   Request 85
          3.2   Queer re-reading of the story of David and Jonathan 85
          3.3   Resonances 90
          3.4   Conclusion 91
      4 Naming ceremony in the context of transitions 92
          4.1   Request 93
          4.2   Queer re-reading of the story of the Ethiopian eunuch 94
          4.3   Resonances 96
          4.4   Conclusion 97
      5 Queer funeral services 98
          5.1   Request 98
          5.2   Queer re-reading of John 8:12 101
          5.3   Resonances 101
          5.4   Conclusion 102
      6 Conclusions 102

VII Queer-affirming pastoral preaching 103
      1 "Get up and walk!" – The healing at the pool of Bethesda
         told from a queer perspective 104
          1.1   Sermon 104
          1.2   Resonances 107
      2 "Come out!" – The raising of Lazarus told from a queer perspective 108
          2.1   Sermon 108
          2.2   Resonances 113
      3 "Zacchaeus and the shame" – The story of the tax collector
         told from a queer perspective 114
          3.1   Sermon 114
          3.2   Resonances 117
      4 "Losing and finding again" – The story of the Prodigal Son
         told from a queer perspective 117
          4.1   Sermon 117
          4.2   Resonances 118
      5 "Out of the Box!" – Beyond pigeonholes told from a queer
         perspective 118
          5.1   Sermon 118
          5.2   Resonances 120
      6 "You shall be a blessing!" – Blessings told from a queer perspective 120
          6.1   Sermon 120
          6.2   Resonances 123
      7 "Jacob, Rachel, Leah & Co." – Family dispute in the house
         of Jacob told from a queer perspective 124

	7.1 Sermon	124
	7.2 Resonances	129
8	Conclusions	129

INTERPRETATION 131

VIII Queer-affirming pastoral theology of diversity 131

1. Queer-affirming pastoral care – Requirements for the pastoral caregiver 131
2. Queer-affirming pastoral care – Interpreting life in light of biblical stories 132
3. Queer-affirming pastoral care – Reciprocal relational events 134
4. Queer-affirming pastoral care – Activating personal strengths 135
5. Queer-affirming pastoral care – Language school for self-worth and social action 136
6. Queer-affirming pastoral care – An innovative driver for welcoming and inclusive congregations 137
7. Queer-affirming pastoral theology of diversity – Life-oriented, creative and transformative 138

Glossary 141

(Self-)reflection questions for queer-affirming pastoral care 145

Safe(r) space checklist – "Safe(r) Spaces" in Pastoral Care 147

Literature 149

Examples of international queer-affirming religious networks 151

Thank you 152

INTRODUCTION

The book is structured into five steps: Classification (Chapter I), Perception (Chapters II–III), Understanding (Chapters IV–V), Implementation (Chapters VI–VII) and Interpretation (Chapter VIII). I will use the first chapter to clarify my concept of pastoral care and to put it in the context of basic queer-theological assumptions. In the second chapter, I will then introduce the social and religiopolitical context of the topic. In Chapter Three, I will describe and summarize the challenges and opportunities for pastoral care in a queer context, with the help of five anonymous case studies from my pastoral care practice. From these, I will propose case-based insights for queer-affirming pastoral care in Chapter Four.

In Chapter Five I will comment on the popular observations made with reference to the so-called "clobber passages", i.e. biblical passages that are weaponized against queer people in order to devalue or condemn them. This is a necessary step in queer-affirming pastoral care, as care seekers often struggle to put them into context. After that, I will use the sixth chapter to summarize pastoral care actions taken in ceremonial services in a queer context, which I experienced as a congregational pastor and later as a pastor at the "Protestant Scholarship Foundation" "Evangelisches Studienwerk" in Villigst/Germany. In the process, I will describe five case studies: a blessing ceremony for a same-sex couple, a baptism for a rainbow family, confirmation classes with the coming out of a teenage participant, a naming ceremony in the context of a transition and a funeral service for a gay man. I will then reflect on the significance of pastoral work in the context of queer-affirming ceremonial services. In the seventh chapter, I will present seven sermons that I have provided in different contexts and that have initiated or supported queer-affirming pastoral care work. I will follow this up by adding further insights and comments I received in response to these sermons. The eighth chapter will be used to formulate conclusions and basic requirements for queer-affirming pastoral care, before finally offering some key proposals for a queer-affirming pastoral theology of diversity. The main part of the book is followed up by a glossary, (self-) reflective questions on queer-affirmative counseling, a checklist for safer spaces, a bibliography, as well as a selection of international queer-affirming and religious networks.

All Bible texts are taken from the King James Bible Online and from translations of the German Revised Lutheran Bible of 2017 or from translations of the German "Bible Edition in Inclusive Language". In addition, I have also supplied some translations of my own.

I understand this book as a written reflection on my pastoral care practice from a queer-theological perspective. I refer to good practice examples from more than twenty years of pastoral care work, from instances where I believe something more can be learned above and beyond the individual case study in question. Of course, there have been counseling sessions that did not succeed for various reasons, or where I reached my own limitations from a professional perspective, and had to refer pastoral care seekers to specialized professionals. It is a book derived from practice, made for practice. In this sense, I hope that it will invite those active in pastoral care, whether it is on a full-time, part-time or voluntary basis, to counsel joyfully, and for the benefit of themselves and others, in a queer-affirming way.

CLASSIFICATION

I What is pastoral care?

1 Approaching pastoral care

Physical accompaniment

The risen Jesus accompanied two disciples to Emmaus. They did not recognize him. Jesus listened to them, talked to them and shared part of the journey with them. He took their worries and needs seriously and perceived their insecurities. Jesus ate and drank with them and finally shared bread and wine with them. This is how he had done it before, so that the two disciples could finally recognize him. The scales fell from their eyes. Jesus was back. How could they not have recognized him before? He had risen from the dead, hallelujah! Through the encounter with the resurrected Jesus, they gained new courage. After Jesus had disappeared again, they went back to Jerusalem to tell the others about their joyful experience.

This biblical story from Luke 24 lays the basis for my thoughts on pastoral care. In this sense, pastoral care is bodily accompaniment along the way, involving attentive listening and participation in both small and large concerns and crises, for a limited period of time, and in very different everyday situations. Asking questions and being silent, listening and providing company, were decisive interventions made by the risen Jesus. He also reactivated memories of the disciples, by sharing the communion with them. Through the familiar ritual, he released inner sources of strength in the disciples and changed their view of the future, so that hope rather than despair shaped their perspective on life.

Considering a person holistically – body, spirit and soul

In my understanding, pastoral care means seeing and addressing a person holistically – body, spirit, and soul. It is G*d who made them unique and full of wonders (acc. to Ps. 139,14) and it is in their wholeness that they become G*d's image. That is why empathy and appreciation for all are non-negotiable prerequisites for pastoral care. Understanding and recognizing people in their complexity and uniqueness is only possible, though, when they are seen within the context of their family structures, social systems, and sociopolitical connections, which in turn can only be done by considering their humanity.

In so doing, psychological and psychosocial insights are equally as relevant as systemic, socioeconomic, gender-sensitive considerations – and maybe even intercultural and interreligious ones. In a pastoral context, that means considering the self-identification and worldview of the person seeking guidance, as well as treating their self-interpretation with respect – all while non-judgementally accepting that their views may well differ from one's own. This mode of pastoral care needs to be sensitive to differences and requires "interpathy" (a term coined by the US-American pastoral care worker David Augsburger) in addition to the concept of empathy (see Augsburger 1986, p. 27–32). Interpathy means relinquishing one's own views for a limited period of time, in order to substantially enlarge them later by adding the views of others.

Meaningfulness and interpretation of life

Individuals seeking counsel in pastoral care are seen as "simul iustus et peccator" or "simultaneously just and sinful people." In the counseling process, they soon realize that this ambivalence has been a genuine part of the Protestant perspective on humanity since Martin Luther. This insight can significantly relieve pressure and stress, thus enabling a more relaxed approach within the framework of a meeting. If in the face of pain, challenges and crises G*d's words can resonate through biblical storytelling, symbols, psalms or prayers, G*d's loving acceptance and justification of people "through grace alone" becomes tangible. And it is in that moment that individuals seeking advice feel enabled to address feelings of guilt and shame and to name their own mistakes. Human lives and G*d's salvation history forge a connection that resonate with each other. As a result, Christian pastoral care views people within the framework of their potential, as humans standing before G*d instead of reducing them to their limitations. Sources of strength, inner resources, and potential courses of action come into play, enabling their development in pastoral spaces. In that sense, pastoral care work always offers guidance, meaningfulness, and an interpretation of life in the face of adversity.

Where does pastoral care take place?

Pastoral care can take place in short everyday conversations in the street, in the supermarket or outside the church doors. It happens in children and youth work, in schools, at parent-teacher evenings, with those preparing for their confirmation, or in conversations with young people in general. Pastoral care has its fixed place in the life of the congregation, be it at baptisms, weddings, funerals and bereavement care, at birthday celebrations, or in meetings with the elderly, the sick, the dying, and their relatives. However, pastoral care also takes place as part of inter-congregational socio-diaconal work with the unemployed and the homeless, as well as in work with migrants, people from the LGBTQI+ community, people who are HIV-positive, addicts, and other social groups. Finally, specialized pastoral care is a field on its own. It takes place in specific places such as hospitals, universities and colleges, schools, psychiatric wards, prisons, retirement homes, airports or hospices. Pastoral care in the parish is neither more nor less important, neither better nor worse than pastoral care offered for instance in a hospital or a psychiatry unit. The different locations where pastoral care takes place cannot be pitted against one another.

How does pastoral care happen?
Pastoral care is a holistic and interactive communication process. It is characterized by verbal, non-verbal and dynamic parts. All the senses are involved. The process opens up a space for pain and grief, but also for joy, gratitude and other feelings, thereby offering a protective space as well. Especially in end-of-life conversations, with grieving relatives or with traumatized people, silence or non-verbal gestures, facial expressions, haptics (touch) and ritual acts play an important role. Liturgical lament, prayer, psalm reading, singing and acts of blessing may be included. The flow of energy through the laying on of hands and gestures of blessing, touching and even hugging are possible, but may only be offered gently to those seeking advice, and under no circumstances should they be imposed on them. It is equally important to be present in the counseling encounter, to bear raw feelings and grief, to absorb topics (containment), to release resources (coping) and not to over-dissect feelings and experiences. And sometimes, when there are simply no more words left, it is a matter of sharing silence with the person seeking counsel in the face of unspeakable pain.

At the same time, the counselor may fall prey to being overly prescriptive, giving unsolicited advice, exceeding their own limitations, overestimating their own abilities or going way beyond the original remit. Prudence, humility and acknowledgement of one's own limitations help with the responsible organization of counseling sessions. For this reason, pastoral care workers regularly reflect on their roles and limitations within supervision settings.

At this point, I would once again like to stress what is most important to me: pastoral care means perceiving the individual person with the eyes of G*d and through the eyes of others, as this creates space and hope for development and change.

2 My personal position

Concern for the well-being of the people who seek pastoral care drives me as a pastoral counselor. My desire that they may be well in body, mind and soul has accompanied me in my work for over twenty years. At the same time, I seek to promote the biblical message of liberation from injustice and oppression. Biblical stories reveal the stories of those who have suffered, or who have been marginalized or excluded. I am convinced that this message is still relevant today. Therefore, it is important to me that chaplains exercise vigilance, especially towards those who are threatened, discriminated against or marginalized. Often these are old or sick people, socially marginalized people, people of different backgrounds and ethnicities, those who are physically/mentally impaired and/or queer people. Their experiences are of central importance to me from a theological point of view. And to me their everyday issues and concerns represent central challenges for theology and pastoral care.

In this book, I focus on the situation of queer people who also identify as believers or spiritual. Many of them have had to endure exclusionary and humiliating experiences in church settings. They were, and still are, disparagingly viewed as second-class Christians in some places, especially in (right-wing) evangelical circles of all denominations (see Schulz 2022, pp. 76–80; for further life-history examples also see Platte, 2018). Their way of life or their gender identity denote them as 'people living in sin', who do not fit in, or who allegedly disturb the peace of the church.

Changing the attitude towards their concerns, issues and desires is a central theological task for me, rather than a marginal side issue. This perspective has accompanied me ever since I became first involved in liberation theologies during my theology studies.[1] All of these approaches – within liberation theologies – are contextual theologies. Their content must always be related concretely and in close proximity to everyday life, within the relevant context and without general validity. It is in using these theological approaches that I learned to work theologically in a context-sensitive and concrete way. Audre Lorde, Katie Cannon, Sarah Vecera and others have taught me not to pit issues of racism, colonialism, homophobia and transphobia against each other, but to include

---

1   I was especially interested in feminist liberation theologies (see Schüssler-Fiorenza 1988; Schottroff 1990). However, these approaches often fell short with regard to the question of different forms of life and sexualities. Therefore, I studied lesbian-feminist-liberation theologies such as Carter Heyward's book (1989) and later queer approaches in theology. Marcella Althaus-Reid has influenced me in a special way (see Althaus-Reid 2000, 2003).

their structural and intersectional interconnectedness within my theological reflections (see Vecera 2022; Lorde 1984/2021).²

The concepts that have become especially important for me over the past twenty years have been those that have broadened the focus on social privilege, skin color, and gender justice in the context of the so-called Global North.³ Such approaches challenge theological positions with regard to gender-sensitive, anti-racist, and postcolonial issues. Queer-theological approaches such as those of Marcela Althaus-Reid, Linn Tonstad, and Patrick Cheng have ultimately enabled me to engage with queer-theological concerns and translate them into the German-speaking context (see Tonstad 2018; Cheng 2011; Althaus-Reid 2000, 2003).

Against this background, I am interested in a theology and pastoral care that allows queer people to speak in their daily contexts and to have their voices heard. For a long time, they have only been the topic of theological debates rather than participants. It is now time to take them seriously in theology and pastoral care as subjects and experts on their own life stories and to listen to them. To this end, I explore what conditions must be met in pastoral care so that queer people can accept pastoral care without fear and while feeling safe and respected.

In this respect, theological and pastoral work is not a neutral occupation for me, but rather one of accompanying those who have suffered injustice or pain in a spirit of solidarity. When they come to me for counseling, I listen to them attentively and take them seriously as subjects of their own life story.

The goal is to bolster the resources and resilience of those seeking pastoral care so that they can discover and learn to implement action plans that will strengthen them in the tension between personal challenges and structural circumstances.

3 Biblical-theological basic assumptions

In my experience, biblical stories can have an important meaning in queer-affirming counseling – especially because queer people have often only experienced biblical texts when used as a weapon against them. Yet the Bible has a central overall message: G*d is with the oppressed and marginalized. G*d sides with them. The core of G*d's proclamation is the healing of unholy conditions and relationships, as well as the peaceful coexistence of all people. Whether in the great biblical narratives, or within smaller passages of Scripture, this mes-

---

2   Antiracist and womanist liberation theologians lamented white feminists' lack of engagement with racism and privilege (see, e.g., Cannon 1988).
3   The theologian Sarah Vecera was the first to spell this out theologically in a German context (see Vecera 2022).

sage prevails – and that despite, or perhaps even because, biblical texts are enormously diverse or even contradictory in themselves. The texts cover a period of many centuries and reflect very different cultural, socio-political and economic conditions – which is why biblical texts can only be read and understood within their linguistic/etymological and historical context. Nevertheless, an overall message runs through all the books of the Bible: the texts are directed against oppressive structures and stand up for holistic well-being (shalom) and a life worth living for all. The focus on upright and respectful coexistence is also central to pastoral care. In the following, I will mention some other significant aspects of biblical stories.

Listening without reservations

Jesus allowed himself to be approached and invited, without reservations, by so-called outsiders, thus giving signals that are decisive for my understanding of pastoral care. Jesus visited people regardless of their origin, skin color, gender identity and social status. He listened to them, ate and drank with them, took their life stories seriously and considered their resources in order to alleviate their ailments or change their circumstances for suffering, and thereby transform their lives. Jesus was both interlocutor and advocate, role model and initiator of change. He confronted rigid doctrines and spoke out in favor of a people-centered coexistence. He made those on the margins the center of his attention and criticized complacency.

In 2016 I published a poem on these thoughts on my website. It is called: "Without Reservations" (Söderblom 2016):

Without reservations
"I invite you!" (Matthew 9:9–12)
Jesus lets the tax collector be the host.
He accepts with pleasure. Eats and drinks with him.
    What, him? But he's horrible! A cutthroat!
Jesus enjoys what is offered to him without further questions.
He shares the meal with the outsider.
    What, him? But he's horrible! A cutthroat!
Jesus knows: Those who meet the other without reservations can be surprised.
Each and anyone deserves a chance.
    What, him? But he's horrible! A cutthroat!
Jesus is not interested in the protest. Others are outraged.
    Why doesn't Jesus eat with us? Why with this outsider?
Jesus speaks to all.

He takes them from the margins to the center. He includes the marginalized.
He reinstates the seemingly useless, the strangers and others with their dignity.
What, him? But he's horrible! A cutthroat!
Jesus meets the lonely, the strangers, the sick, and the outsiders.
He does not condemn them. Instead, he listens to them, takes them seriously,
wants to understand their story. He does not label,
does not pigeonhole, does not exclude.
Everyone deserves a chance.
Because you can meet G*d through every human being.

*Seeing G*d's image in the other person*
G*d created human beings male and female and everything in between, just as G*d created light and darkness with dawn and dusk and everything else in between; just as G*d created water and solid land with bogs, marshes and swamps and everything else in between, G*d also created the animals in the water, in the fields, and in the air, and all other living beings in between. Although the Creation Story only uses dualistic juxtapositions due to the poetic structure of the text, they encompass all phenomena and creatures in between. And everything and everyone in between also belong, including non-binary, trans* or intersex persons, because according to biblical testimony, every human being is made in G*d's image (Genesis 1:27 f.).

Each and every one is unique, an original before G*d and blessed by G*d. As Martin Luther put it, this blessing is awarded to every human being without any advance performance, "by grace alone". By grace alone, every human being is granted unrestricted dignity. At the same time, G*d establishes human beings as governors of the whole creation on earth in the first creation account. In other words, G*d trusts humans to act ethically and with ecological responsibility. G*d expects humans to be mindful and respectful of creation and all of its constituent parts, instead of ruthlessly plundering, polluting or destroying creation.

Accordingly, the Christian view of humankind and the world belong together. They are shaped and supported by G*d's promise and blessing. Both encourage and empower us to deal responsibly and mindfully with each other and the whole of creation, to live together in harmony. Alongside this encouragement, is the requirement to fashion this responsibility within a prudent, ecologically mindful and peaceful framework. In the event of crises, problems and emergencies, this attitude entails being collectively and individually vigilant and standing up for one another. And it is precisely this attitude that is also significant within Christian-based pastoral care.

Relating the concept of liberation from oppression

Where people are oppressed, where they suffer injustice and violence, where they are marginalized or deprived of their rights, G*d's liberating message applies to them. It is the same promise that G*d gave to Moses, Miriam, Aaron and the whole people of Israel in the book of Exodus. In essence, G*d spoke to Moses at that time like this: Leave slavery and look for another place, a just and peaceful one, where you can live free from oppression.

I will be with you. I will accompany you by day and by night and give you guidance. But protect the old, the widows and the strangers! For you yourselves were strangers in Egypt (Exodus 3).

G*d's promise and commands are inseparably linked. They involve both encouragement and empowerment to take responsibility. Unjust conditions are to be abandoned or changed through social, Christian and socio-political commitment in such a way that people change from being affected to being involved, from being objects to being subjects of their life story and their living environment. For this, people need just socio-political conditions, participation, security, healthy nutrition and education. This also includes physical, mental and spiritual support. Thus, diaconia and spiritual care, everyday proclamation and community action, share a task that can only succeed through wise and prudent interactions.

Living the Body of Christ

According to Pauline understanding (Romans 12:4–6; 1 Corinthians 12:12–27), people with their different life experiences, ways of life, abilities and talents all belong to the one Body of Christ. It is only together that the Body of Christ can be the living embodiment of Christian life and radiate it in a credible way. Nevertheless, its members are different. They are endowed with different functions, qualities, contexts, life stories and needs, and it is precisely in their diversity that they represent the unity of the Christian community.

For me, this leitmotif is central to perceiving people in their differences, recognizing and welcoming them as equal parts of the Body of Christ. Exclusion, devaluation and condemnation have no part in that. But respect for others, openness and hospitality do play a part, because this is the only way to reach and touch people who have not yet experienced G*d's liberating message – be it within the mainstream church or beyond. Those who live differently, speak a different language, have a different skin color, have knowledge of very different sacred writings and symbols – they all are seekers and pilgrims on their life's journey. By turning Christian meeting places into resting places and shelters, where people tell each other life stories and learn from each other, the Body of Christ can grow and work internally and externally. In this way, G*d's love for neighbor and enemy alike finds real representation. Pastoral care that takes this image of Christian community into consideration and takes it seriously, actively contributes to people's ability to feel a sense of belonging in both times of joy and suffering – despite or precisely because of their differences.

Baptism knows no gender
"There is no longer Jew nor Christian, there is no longer enslaved nor free, there is no longer male nor female. For you are all one in Christ!" (Gal 3:28).

At this point in Galatians, Paul quotes an older early Christian baptismal formula. In this formula, Greeks and Jews, masters and slaves, women and men are no longer defined by social, cultural or religious roles, but all are called together to follow Christ without distinction of position or status. Not only was this a vision of the future, but it also became a norm-transcending activity that would distinguish the first Christian communities. Within these communities at least, all gender, religious and class differences were considered to be overcome through baptism – the mere act itself creating heavenly conditions on earth, in a very real, concrete, and tangible way. This original Christian baptismal formula (still) forms an important base for the gender-sensitive considerations of today.

"For you are all one in Christ and heirs of the promise!" continues Paul (Gal 3:29). The power of baptism, effected by the Holy Spirit, overcame norms and boundaries then, and it still invites us to do so today.

Called to freedom
"To freedom you have been called!" – states the letter to the Galatians (Gal 5:13). This is no arbitrary call to freedom, though, but to the freedom to testify to G*d's love in very different voices, images and stories, to pass it on and to live by it. In so doing, people open up spaces to live their lives in a spirit of care and respect. For me, this means being mindful of oneself and others and acting in a resource-oriented way, to respect each other without patronizing, to support each other without encroaching on another, and to create and protect spaces for a happy and colorful togetherness.

The goal is to walk a little of the way together, to accompany those seeking pastoral care as they face obstacles, and to make it possible to experience the liberating message of the Gospel. Dogmatic teaching has no place here. It is about making G*d's promise tangible and passing on G*d's love. For G*d's promise was first given to people by G*d, without people having to do anything to earn it.

Activating power, love, and prudence
"G*d has not given us the spirit of fear, but of power, love and prudence" (2 Tim. 1:7).

If counselors can both bring strength, love and caution into their sessions and draw from them as resources, they will have a good spiritual toolkit at their disposal, in addition to humility and faith in G*d, even when they are overcome by doubt and despair. Death and dying, injustice, illness and distress are topics regularly encountered by pastoral care givers, which makes building up one's own personal resources and resilience important. Reflecting on one's own role, as well as on personal and professional boundaries, is a permanent feature of all pastoral care.

4 Approaching queer-theological research

"Queer" is a derogatory term, a slur initially used to describe and reduce homosexual women and men to their sexualities or gender identities. Since the 1980s and 90s, the term has increasingly been reclaimed by the LGBTQI+ community, transforming it into a source of strength. "Queer" is now used by people positioning themselves outside of heteronormative categories, with regard to sexualities, lifestyles and/or non-conformity to the gender binary. It consciously pushes the envelope, challenging norms and categories, adding fluidity to the mix.

As such, queer theologies are not a theological discipline as much as they are an umbrella for different perspectives in theological research. They mirror the realities of individuals experiencing exclusion and rejection based on their sexual orientation, their non-binary identities or their otherness, making queer theologies contextual and specific in the process. They embody critical approaches and a plurality of perspectives.

Queer research perspectives are aimed at questioning seemingly self-evident heteronormative and cis-normative notions of sexuality and gender identities and crossing borders, i.e. "queering" them (see Söderblom 2020b, pp. 146–150). In so doing, patriarchal power structures and hegemonic images of masculinity are also exposed (see Söderblom (2009, p. 71 ff.).

In queer-theological approaches, sexual diversity and diverse gender identities are no longer defensively justified, but taken for granted (cf. Tonstad 2018). Therefore the focus is no longer on the few biblical passages that comment on same-sex sexual practices. (These so-called "clobber passages" can be found in Leviticus 18:22; Leviticus 20:13; Deuteronomy 23:17; Romans 1:18–32; 1 Corinthians 6:9–10; and 1 Timothy 1:9–10.) Through a queer-theological lens, these texts are predominantly seen in the context of prostitution, pederasty, and sexual contacts between married men at that time. Most biblical scholars and exegetical researchers do not consider them meaningful as a context for lesbian, gay, and bisexual forms of relationships of the 21st century (see Plisch 2016, pp. 23–31; Lings 2013; Greenough 2020, pp. 97–100).

Instead, they understand people as being made in G*d's image (Genesis 1:27 f.), thus guaranteeing the uniqueness and dignity of all people – regardless of origin, skin color, age, physical ability, gender identity, and sexual orientation. Diverse lifestyles, sexualities and gender identities are viewed from the standpoint of the biblical double commandment to love (Mark 12:29 ff.; Matthew 22:34–40; Luke 10:25–28) both neighbor and oneself. This commandment of G*d to love both neighbor and self does not distinguish between individuals. It calls on everyone individually and collectively to respect and accept the other.

Social, cultural, and linguistic historical research has also been advanced by queer-theological approaches, with hermeneutic changes in perspective practiced. This work is called a queer re-reading of biblical texts.

Queer biblical interpretations consciously conduct biblical exegesis and hermeneutics from a queer perspective (see Söderblom 2020a, pp. 11–73). They use linguistic complexity, literary interstices, the unsaid and the empty spaces in biblical texts, to point out the creative act of interpretation in every Bible reading. They consciously frame their interpretive perspectives as intersubjective meaningful spaces between ancient biblical texts and queer contexts of the 21st century, queer-brushing biblical texts in an undogmatic and provocative way, while examining them for ambiguous representations of bodies and gender. Homoerotic hints in biblical texts are tracked down and contextualized. The results of queer re-readings and research are then interdisciplinarily and intersectionally linked to findings from other research fields (such as studies into anti-Semitism, colonialism and poverty) and related to each other (see Söderblom 2021a, p. 167 f.).

PERCEPTION

II Context

1 "Outside the box"[4]

For many within church environments, lesbian, gay, bisexual, trans*, inter*, and queer people (LSBTQI+) in Germany still live outsiders' lives, because they consider their lives and gender identities outside "the box" of the norm. However, a lot has changed in the Protestant regional churches in Germany over the past 30 years. Most regional churches will now marry or at least bless lesbian and gay couples in church services (see Verband der Evangelischen Studierendengemeinden in Deutschland 2019, pp. 13–16). LGBTQI+ pastors need not fear for their jobs any longer, if they decide to live openly in a non-heterosexual relationship, or if their gender identity does not fit the gender binary. That does not mean, though, that issues related to diverse lifestyles or gender identities have vanished.

Heated debates, especially around biblical passages that broach the issue of homosexuality, are still very common and have hardly changed in terms of argumentation. Attitudes toward biblical interpretation and conclusions drawn remain controversial as well.

2 Learning paths

Nevertheless, the church as an organization has learned a few things from the debates held over the past thirty years. Since the 1980s, almost every Protestant church in Germany has held regional and state church synods (church parliaments) to discuss and argue the assessment and handling of different sexual orientations and gender identities. The issues have been debated back

---

4 This chapter is an updated and revised excerpt from an article I first published in the online magazine futur2 (see Söderblom 2020c).

and forth and then placed in the hands of theological committees. Church boards and church groups have taken polls. The Protestant Church in Germany (EKD) as well as the regional churches have published, hotly debated and revised statements and guidelines, and then debated them all over again. The whole issue seemed to be stuck in a never-ending loop of discussion, without producing anything close to a change of position. It was not until committees and synods started listening to full-time and volunteer LGBTQI+ employees, instead of speaking *about* them, that the pattern was broken and something began to shift. Since then, a variety of transformational processes have been witnessed in this area.

3 #OutInChurch

The pace of change has also increased in the Roman Catholic Church in Germany in recent years.[5] The rate of change has sped up dramatically over the past three years in particular: in May 2021, blessing ceremonies were held in over one hundred Catholic parishes throughout Germany under the banner #LiebeGewinnt (LoveWins), which explicitly invited same-sex couples to receive a blessing. In January 2022, the documentary "Wie Gott uns schuf: Coming-out in der katholischen Kirche" (As G*d made us: Coming out in the Roman Catholic Church) was broadcast on ARD after 125 Catholic Christians came out as queer as part of the campaign #OutInChurch. Some of them featured in the documentary. The campaign was flanked by a broad social media event, during which all participants chose to show their faces in photos and used a headline sentence to communicate why they were participating in the #OutInChurch campaign (cf. Brinkschröder/Ehebrecht-Zumsande/Gräwe/Mönkebüscher/Werner 2022; see also Gräwe/Johannemann/Klein 2021). Since January 2022, over 300 queer Roman Catholic Christians have also joined the campaign. This type of public coverage of the topic is unprecedented for the Roman Catholic Church in Germany. In response, various dioceses signaled that those involved in the campaign need not fear any consequences under labor law. At the same time, the establishment of queer-affirming pastoral care services is progressing in the dioceses. The Diocese of Mainz, for instance, officially appointed two pastoral theologians for rainbow pastoral care in April 2022 (see Diocese of Mainz 2022). The Roman Catholic Church Days held at the end of

---

5   The catalog of the exhibition "Give me my Rights!" covers the situation of queer believers in the Roman Catholic Church worldwide through autobiographical testimonies (see Ökumenische Arbeitsgruppe Homosexuelle und Kirche (HuK) e.V. 2018).

May 2022 in Germany, also gave individuals from #OutInChurch significant coverage on several panels and across other formats, thereby creating further publicity for the topic.

Nevertheless, in many Christian congregations, it is still not possible for church employees to openly live their lives, whatever the denomination. They do not come out for fear of rejection and prejudice. Too many of them have experienced exclusion and humiliation in their lives, especially in church environments, when choosing to come out. This has often resulted in telling stressful white lies and leading double lives (see Lesben- und Schwulenverband Deutschland (LSVD) 2021). In other places, however, full-time and voluntary activists are now able to go about their work completely unaffected by the issue.

4 Pluralization of sexual orientations, life forms and gender identities

Dealing with the above-mentioned areas has become more relaxed in many places. Encounters with real-life LGBTQI+ employees and volunteers in congregations and church institutions in particular have shown rejection and reservations to diminish over time, when people meet or work together in everyday life. Once prejudice meets real-life people face to face and preconceived ideas are replaced by concrete experiences, many of these fears dissipate.

Openly lesbian, gay, and bisexual parishioners, pastors, and church staff have changed the attitudes of church leaders and many parishioners with their presence over the past thirty years (see Söderblom 2013). In their wake, trans* pastors and employees have also begun to be more open about their transition in the church environment. As a result, matters of gender identity have become more visible and are being discussed in many more places.[6] There are an increasing number of "rainbow families" – lesbian, gay or queer couples who live as blended families with children in their parsonage/vicarage or church environment. Admittedly, there remain problems and reservations and conflicts to be overcome here as well. But we also witnessed increasing incidences of rainbow families being warmly welcomed into church life. Albeit delayed, a diversity of lifestyles and a softening of the gender binary are becoming more and more evident in church environments.

---

6 For example Elke Spörkel, who was the protagonist of the documentary "When Mr. Reverend becomes Mrs. Reverend: Elke fights for her parish". The documentary was broadcast on ARD on July 26, 2020 (see also Schreiber 2016; Lüdtke 2017; EKHN 2018; Wolfrum 2019).

5 Role models for self-acceptance

The most important step in this transformative process came about by the refusal of those affected to be portrayed solely as 'problem cases' in an otherwise heteronormative and binary world. Instead, they self-confidently showed (the majority) that the opening up of churches and church spaces for LGBTQI+ people led to church institutions and congregations becoming more colorful, joyful, and humane places. Furthermore, they proved that LGBTQI+ pastors and church employees who live their lives openly with all their various gender identities, represent a model in lived self-acceptance (see Häneke 2019). This is because those who are open about themselves in congregations have already reflected on the complex and often difficult relationship between faith, gender identity and sexuality and have taken a stand on it. In this way, they can act as encouraging role models for young people in search of their gender identity and their own way of doing faith and life.[7]

LGBTQI+ people in church congregations and church institutions offer important resources in regard to coexistence:
- Body knowledge: what it is like to feel different and to exist on the fringes. This knowledge teaches sensitivity, mindfulness, and appreciation for anyone who feels insecure or uprooted.
- Experiential knowledge about minority life: This knowledge teaches us to pay respect and attention to someone regardless of skin color, origin, age, gender identity, sexual orientation, and physical ability.
- Stress knowledge relating to white lies and double lives: This knowledge warns us against approaching others with self-righteous arrogance and by exerting moral pressure, but listening and perceiving them without judgement.

People with this experiential knowledge clearly convey that nothing about them is deficient or wrong, but that they, like everyone else, are images of G*d. In this way, they provide basic theological education by virtue of their own experiences.

---

7   For instance the YouTube channel "Anders Amen" created by two lesbian pastors Ellen and Stefanie Radtke from Eime in Lower Saxony, which has been around since 2019 (https://www.youtube.com/channel/UC8GQAXuJ_DpNg6hu1HHM73w).

6 Respectful pastoral care as an initial spark for commitment

LGBTQI+ adolescents and young adults in particular are still afraid to come out at school, university, at their place of vocational training or within their peer group. They fear gloating, insults or even violence; the suicide rate within this cohort remains many times higher than among heterosexual youth (see Schinzler 2018; Söderblom 2015, pp. 259–270). However, when young people see that lesbian or gay pastors or non-binary pastors and church staff are self-confident regarding their sexual orientation or gender identity, and at the same time respected in the congregation, this is encouraging for many. They realize that being different is not bad or wrong. This is also true in Christian university congregations. Feedback from those seeking advice shows that the fear threshold is lower for them to approach queer pastors, to come to them during office hours and talk about their problems, as they neither fear moral preaching nor punishment. In this way, pastoral care can often offer preventative measures. Teenagers and young adults are encouraged to stand up for themselves and it is not uncommon for them to become involved in community activities and queer-affirming projects later.

From my own pastoral practice, I know that it is not only significant for young queer people to know about LGBTQI+ pastors and staff, though. Many students and adults who are struggling with their sexuality or gender identity, or who are otherwise searching for guidance, will also prefer to approach someone they consider open, appreciative, and undogmatic. Those who are afraid of being considered sick or sinful in a conversation, will not open up. On the other hand, those who have positive experiences in church and feel welcome there, are motivated to come back and get involved. In other words, it is interesting for more than one reason to gain a more precise understanding of what queer-affirming pastoral care is, how it can be implemented in different contexts, and what impact it has on pastoral-theological considerations as a whole. And this is exactly what I want to do here.

III Case studies

In this chapter, I will describe five pastoral care situations, in which I was involved as a university chaplain from 2020 to 2022, in the form of condensed case studies.[8] In order to preserve the pastoral confidentiality (see EKD 2009), all examples

---

8   On university chaplaincy as a whole see the "Handbuch Studierendenseelsorge" by Hirschberg/Freudenberg/Plisch (2022); more specifically on the topic of "different life plans and gender justice in university chaplaincy", see Ritter/Plisch (2022).

have been anonymized and any identifiable biographical information removed. The quotations in the case studies (marked in italics) are taken from notes I made following the pastoral care interviews. They are not literally transcriptions, but reconstructions from memory. They contain edits and thematic links. These are consciously accepted, since they show the interconnectedness of the pastor with the events. Consequently, the case studies merely reflect my subjective memory of the conversations.

1 Case study: "I don't know how to say it!"

1.1 Meeting

It was a Wednesday afternoon. I was preparing for an evening service and a counseling session was coming up in fifteen minutes, when there was a knock at the door. J., a chemistry student, opened my office door. She was wearing a mask and stopped on the threshold. She knew she was early. I asked her to wait on our leather sofa in the second-floor hallway until I shut down my computer. During the Covid period, we offered primarily online counseling or "Walk-and-Talk-meetings." From the preliminary phone conversation, it was clear, though, that neither would be appropriate here. So, I put on a pot of coffee, filled two glasses with water, put cookies and chocolate on a plate, and unlocked the seminar room. (That's where our face to face counseling sessions took place during the pandemic years because it provided enough space). The student took a seat at the large table across from me, thanked me for the water and coffee, and took off her mask. She drank from the glass of water and then held on to it with both hands. Beads of sweat gathered on her forehead.

"Talking is not easy for me. I don't even know how to start,"
she managed with difficulty.

"Don't worry, I have time! Why don't you take a deep breath first? You don't need to order your thoughts either. Just let the words come!" I replied and looked at her encouragingly.

Secure framework: Confidentiality
She took a deep breath. *"Everything we say here stays between us, right?"*
I confirmed to her that the conversation was subject to confidentiality.

She swallowed, took another deep breath and began: *"I think I'm a lesbian and I'm afraid to tell my parents. And in my shared apartment, I don't know how to tell the others either! Everything has to stay between us, otherwise I'll freak out!"*

I nodded understandingly.

Finally being allowed to tell – with someone listening
Over the next half hour, I asked questions, listened attentively, encouraged her to continue, and gradually learned bits and pieces of her story: she had been active in a free church congregation as a teenager, which had shaped her spiritual life. Her parents had started taking her to the free church at an early age. She actually felt comfortable there, but even before she graduated from high school, she had a feeling that she didn't fit into the community in certain ways. She didn't want to get married and have children. She didn't want to just be good and do "woman things" as she called it. She wanted to travel, have adventures, be independent. Now a fourth-semester chemistry major, she had loosely kept in touch with her home congregation. Then, a few weeks ago, she had fallen in love with another student. Since then, her life had been turned upside down.

Naming fears and finding understanding
J. took a deep breath and continued: *"Actually, it's great that I've fallen in love. It tingles in my stomach and everywhere else. But I feel guilty and fear that my parents or someone from my congregation might find out! I am a woman and I have fallen in love with another woman. I can't do that! That is sinful! Our congregation is very clear on that. What am I supposed to do now?"*

After breathlessly forcing out those last sentences, she swallowed in exhaustion, looked at me and began to cry. I handed her a handkerchief, nodded in understanding and waited. She continued to cry, blew her nose at some point and drank a sip of water.

"I'm just afraid that my whole life will fall apart and everyone will be shocked when I tell them I've fallen in love with a woman!" I nodded and replied that I could well understand her worries. We took our time to look at what her worries were and what a worst-case scenario might look like.

I asked about friends and people within her social circle who were on her side. There was one best friend, who was in the know. She wanted to ask her for support.

Then I calmly replied, *"You are brave and courageous for telling me all this. And you have found words to describe your situation. I congratulate you on that. That's a very important step, even if the fear is there and may remain."*

She replied that she was glad to have voiced what had been troubling her.

"Take your time!" I replied, *"You see, the first steps are the hardest. Everything else comes little by little. You set the pace and the rhythm. And you don't have to say more than you want to or can. Period."*

Relieved, she looked at me and hurried to tell me that she still had many questions and felt insecure and vulnerable. I confirmed to her that I could well understand this, and agreed with her that she could visit me during my office hours every two weeks from now on. Step by step we would then work on her questions and see whether, how and when she wanted to tell someone about her feelings of being in love.

I encouraged her not to rush into anything and to give herself time to adjust to the new situation first. *"Enjoy the time with your girlfriend. And at the same time, I understand your worries!"*

J. smiled, thanked me for the conversation, and said, *"Can you also help me with the Bible passages that deal with homosexuality? I need that for my church."*

"We'll take care of that at a future meeting," I replied.

"For this, please bring along any things you have heard people say in your community on this subject. We'll look at them together and work out how we would respond to this. Okay?"

Speeches against fear

Over the next few weeks, we met regularly. J. told me what she was afraid, when she pictured coming out to parents, congregation, and fellow students. We practiced what she wanted to say to her parents and others by role-playing. We looked at the strengths and resources she could use when she was nervous and insecure, and how she could protect herself. Little by little, she became more fluent in talking about herself and her feelings, and we celebrated every sentence she was able to say to her parents in role play.

New home

Finally, we created a small biblical argumentation tool kit for their free church congregation. I will write more about this in Chapter V.

About half a year later, J. came out to her parents, her roommates and her fellow students. There were mixed reactions. But all in all, she was glad for the most part that she had told them. In addition, there had already been a conversation with someone from the congregation. That had been difficult, but it was a start. In the meantime, J. has reached a point where she no longer feels dependent on the judgement of people in her free church.

"If they don't accept me, I can always leave," she once said defiantly. *"After all, I have found a new home in the university chaplaincy in Mainz!"*

The week before Easter, we looked at an Easter text I had written. It is a queer approach to Easter.

1.2 Queer re-reading of the Easter story

Easter[9]

Pushing away the walls of fear and prejudice.
Rolling away the stones of constraint, sensitivities, narrow boundaries.
To finally dare to show myself, to say I, to be there, to take up space. Just as I am.
Just as G*d created me
and blessed me.

---

9   First published in: Söderblom (2020a, p. 41 f.).

Easter
Out of the grave caves of fixed ideas,
a human being shows himself,
confesses to himself.
Look, that's me!
Wanted and blessed by G*d.

Coming Out
Leaving the confinements of what is considered normal.
What will the neighbors say?
How can you do this to us?
What did we do wrong?
No longer willing
to hide in the closet.

Easter
Someone showed us the way.
He left the realm of violence, hatred and death.
He overcame deadly expectations
and called out to us: Look, I live! You can live, too!

Coming Out
Stepping out of the burrows of prejudice, slander.
Daring to be myself, just as I am,
created by G*d,
lesbian, gay, bi, trans*, inter*, queer,
free from pigeonholes, labels, or seals of normality.
Simply blessed.
Simply me.
Stepping out of the burrows of prejudice.
Not only for Easter.

1.3 Resonances

We read the poem aloud several times. I had printed it out twice, one for J. and one for me. Afterwards, J. circled words that resonated:

"Leaving the confinements," "burrows of prejudice," "daring," "blessed", "without label", "simply me". J. read these words aloud several times and let them resonate. After a while, she explained why they were important to her. She said that the poem showed her how important it is not to think about others, but to look at how you are doing. It showed her how important it is to have air to breathe, and how liberating it is to step out of narrowly set norms and leave everything behind. But the title "Easter" also showed her that everything has its price. After all, Jesus was murdered and buried before being resurrected three days later. Something came to an end on the cross. And then something new came, which was transformational and offered hope. That is what she was experiencing with herself at the moment. Something in her life was coming to an end. She no longer wanted to hide and pretend that everything was simple and normal. Nothing was normal anymore. Everything was different, and she didn't yet know what would happen next. But the relief of getting out of a dusty cave full of masks and lies felt good to her. Until our next meeting, she wrote an Easter poem of her own. It became her transformation poem, which she has carried with her ever since, giving her courage.

2 Case Study: "I separate to find myself again!"

2.1 Meeting

Thursday evening. M., the person seeking pastoral care, is over 65 years old. She is retired and volunteers in a Protestant congregation in Rheinhessen (the region surrounding Mainz, Germany). She sought contact with me as a pastor because she'd come across an announcement for the ecumenical Pride service of both university chaplaincies, the ESG and KHG. She had also noticed the queer-friendly publications on the website of the ESG.

We met in the meeting room of the ESG. Water and tea were on the table, the windows slightly ajar as it was warm outside. Due to the pandemic, we kept our distance by putting two tables between us. We would meet about every six weeks for a year.

M. is divorced and the mother of several children. She has had shorter relationships with women previously. At the time of our first contact, she was in the middle of a separation from a woman. Her goal with me was to work on her boundaries and fears.

Attitude: empathy and appreciation
"I do know that the separation is necessary. But it's so hard to take this step. At my age, people don't break up so easily. I'm afraid that I'll stay alone and not be interesting enough. I'm not that athletic. I can't score with hiking and stuff like that."

From the onset I showed M. that I could well understand her fear of being alone. We took a lot of time to name grief and fears, recognizing how they felt and how they blocked her from acting. M. felt that I understood and acknowledged her fears and stressors. She didn't have to justify herself. She was just allowed to speak her truth and it was okay the way it was.

Change of perspective
After some time, I asked her about other people who were important in her life. As it turned out, she was not that alone after all.

"*I still have my children. They are grown up and they live their own lives. But we are getting along well and I see them often. I also have a grandchild whom I love. And I still have my social contacts. I'm well integrated there.*"

She was amazed at how many people were important in her life.

"*Then I don't really need my complicated relationship.*"

M. began to change her perspective. Previously she hadn't been able to see how many people were around her and how important these social contacts were for her. She had lost sight of them because she had completely focused on the difficult relationship. To see herself as an individual again, and not just as the appendage of another woman, gave her relief and inner freedom.

Resources
Over the next few sessions, we worked on realizing which resources she had to regain her independence. Music, fresh air, and her community involvement gave her strength; she was very clear on that. At the same time, she emphasized: "*My hobbies are important, too. But they aren't a replacement for romantic involvement! And how am I supposed to meet women over the age of 65 who are also into women? That's never going to happen!*"

I could also understand these worries well and voiced that. It was obvious that I could not conjure up a new relationship for her. No one could. But we could put our two heads together to make plans where she could meet other queer women: at events held by the queer bar in Mainz and at queer church services. Maybe M. wanted to volunteer in a queer group in the future? In any case, she didn't feel as at home in the church congregation as she used to.

Queer-friendly meeting places have become quite important for M. in the meantime. She doesn't have a new girlfriend yet, but she feels better about herself and her social environment.

Exercise: Strengthening and holding boundaries
In the months that followed, I accompanied M. in finally separating from the woman who was no longer good for her. We practiced drawing boundaries, utilizing small gestures and clear words in role-play. We talked about agreements, whom she would call and what she wanted to do, instead of meeting with her former partner.

I asked her how she could best draw her boundaries. We practiced holding her boundaries and standing firm.

I asked what people could help her say 'stop'.

"My grandmother comes to mind. She was a strong and very loving person with a mind of her own. I've imagined her before, when I was in a difficult situation."

I asked her in what way she could draw from that source of strength.

"Well, I would put her on my shoulder. Then I have her with me in difficult situations and I can ask her for support. That way I could talk to her as my confidante and protector."

M. practiced this step for the next few weeks. She even put a photo of her grandmother in her purse to look at when she needed support. She was able to separate from her friend and then just walk away, instead of getting involved and entangled in emotional conversations over and over again, as she had done before. I encouraged her in this and celebrated the success with her.

Reinforcement: I am who I am!
She had relapses and ultimately needed more than half a year to make the separation final. But she did it. And most importantly, she went to a queer-friendly bar and volunteered for events.

"I want to do my own thing, I now meet other women and I am active in various groups. I am free and can do what I want. That's good for me!"

In later sessions, we talked about what it meant for her to have come out that late. For a long time M. had the feeling that she was not normal. Not really straight, but not really gay, either. She didn't fit into the queer scene, but she didn't really fit into a conventional Protestant congregation either. She was a mother, divorced, fell in love with women, felt somehow different and didn't fit anywhere.

For a long time, some lesbian friends had continued to regard M. as heterosexual, since she had been married and had children. And in her congregation, some had difficulty with the fact that she had left her husband to be with a woman. As a result, she struggled with guilt and feelings of shame.

We took time for her to name her feelings. I encouraged her to give free rein to her feelings. It helped her to be who she was, despite all the difficulties and the expectations of others. For this, we worked with the biblical story of Jacob and his feelings of guilt and shame.

2.2 Queer re-reading of the story of Jacob

Jacob[10]
Background: Jacob, the son of Rebekah and Isaac, lived in Beersheba, a town in Canaan. He had tricked his father into giving him the firstborn blessing. According to the tradition of the time, this blessing would have gone to his firstborn twin brother Esau. But Jacob wanted that blessing at all costs, because power, livelihood and G*d's protection depended

---

10 First published in: Söderblom (2020a, pp. 65–67).

on it. With the help of his mother Rebekah, Jacob outwitted his father Isaac and convinced him that he was Esau. So, Jacob received the blessing from his father (Genesis 27:28 f.).

When his twin brother Esau learned of the deception, he threatened to slay Jacob. Jacob had to flee and traveled to Aram in the land of the Aramites to be with his relative, Laban of Beersheba. In Aram, he worked for Laban for a total of 14 years and had a total of 12 sons in a polygamously organized extended family with his two wives Leah and Rachel and his maids Bilhah and Zilpah (Genesis 29:1–30:24). Ultimately, he left Laban again with his wives, children, maidservants and his entire livestock (Genesis 31) to return to Canaan.

At the Jabbok
When Jacob embarked on his journey back to his old home, he realized that he would probably meet his brother Esau there. Sensing the potential difficulties, he sent messengers ahead to announce him. The messengers returned and reported that Esau was already on his way to meet him, and with him four hundred men. Jacob became afraid for his life. He divided his family, workers and maids, sheep, goats and camels into two herds and sent them off in different directions to protect at least part of his property from the attack of his brother. Jacob gave the two leaders of his flocks each a large number of gifts for Esau to appease him. He himself stayed behind and spent the night by the river Jabbok.

During the night, an unknown man surprised him. The stranger came out of nowhere. Jacob did not know who he was, nor where he came from. They fought each other all night (Genesis 32:23–33). Neither won the fight. Towards the end, though, the stranger injured Jacob's hip joint so badly that Jacob would limp for the rest of his life. Jacob yelled at the stranger that he would not let him go until he blessed him. The stranger asked Jacob his name and gave him the new name "Israel" ("G*d's warrior"). The stranger himself did not reveal his name, but he blessed Jacob. The latter then called the place of the battle "Penuel" (in the face of G*d), stating that Jacob knew that he had fought with G*d.

Traditional interpretations
In traditional interpretations, it is assumed that Jacob struggled with G*d themselves and that the first fruits blessing previously obtained is finally recognized through G*d's blessing. Jacob emerges from the struggle strengthened, prepared for the encounter with Esau. This is important for traditional interpretations of the Bible, because Jacob – just like Abraham and Isaac – is considered the ancestor of the Davidic lineage and thus the ancestor of Jesus.

Queer re-reading
A re-reading of this biblical passage within a queer interpretational framework allows us to reconstruct a different narrative to this story: Jacob spends the whole night fighting a stranger. The biblical text introduces him as a "man unknown to

Jacob". This duel could be read (homo)erotically: Two men wrestle each other in the mud, body on body. The altercation does not end with one of them being overcome by the other and yet – or maybe for that exact reason – the physical encounter is disturbing and deeply essential. The stranger remains a mystery and defies any attributed gender identity. Although introduced as male, it is his vague appearance that makes him defy a fixed gender category.

As in other interpretations of this story, the queer biblical interpretation identifies the stranger with G*d, yet G*d does not appear here as the absent, distant, forever untouchable entity traditional theologians like to present themselves as. G*d is presented as approachable, touchable, fleshly. G*d is felt, making themselves vulnerable, while remaining a mystery. This re-reading certainly presents G*d as someone who gets their hands dirty and engages in bodily contact with a fellow man.

Fighting guilt and shame
In traditional exegeses, Jacob's struggle with G*d at the Jabbok river is interpreted psychologically – as an inner struggle against feelings of guilt and shame, among other things. It is seen as a journey inward, a struggle against one's own darker side, a struggle against feelings of guilt and shame linked to his deception. This process is not a simple linear path, but a process of life and death – with all its detours, crises and threats. And Jacob survives this struggle.

The struggle for a blessing
From a queer perspective, every coming out process of LGBTQI+ people can also be seen as a physical, mental and spiritual struggle for a life of dignity and recognition. It is a struggle against standardized values in a (hetero)normative environment. And it is a struggle for respect and G*d's blessing.

Against this background, this biblical story reveals a G*d who is quite different. G*d crosses boundaries and forces Jacob to do the same. This G*d is neither male nor female. G*d lets themselves be touched physically and also touches the other. In so doing, G*d destroys the dualistically arranged categories of normality and deviation, body and spirit, subject and object. And when the morning dawns, G*d blesses Jacob.

2.3 Resonances

"Well, I didn't cheat!" M. winked at me. *"I didn't steal anyone's blessing. But I didn't get it either. On the contrary, since coming out, I've been sitting on the fence. And everyone else seems to know better what I should or shouldn't do. What I like about Jacob is he didn't give up, dealt with his life, and took responsibility for his actions. And he fought for G*d's blessing until he finally received it. That impresses and encourages me!"*

We talked about the story for a long time. What M. liked especially was that G*d did not condemn, did not accuse, but met Jacob eye to eye. G*d fought with him and left him changed.

"This G*d is so very different from the images of G*d I heard about before. That is soothing. G*d is not so small-minded. If G*d doesn't fit into any pigeonholes, I don't have to fit either. And G*d does not drop Jacob, although he did not fulfill the ideal image of that time. After all, he had cheated and disregarded regulations and traditions. He simply wanted to be blessed by G*d. I can understand that well. I would also like to be blessed.

With all my quirks and seemingly illogical ways of life. I want to be seen as I am. G*d has blessed Jacob. Then I can be blessed too! Would you bless me?"

We talked a bit longer about what G*d's blessing meant to her. It was an intense exchange. Finally, we agreed that I would bless her at our next meeting. And that's exactly what we did. It became a small blessing ceremony. I lit a rainbow candle, placed a small cross on the table. I had written the Bible verse on a postcard for her and added some personal lines. I gave a short speech on the above Bible passage and summarized our exchange on it. I asked her afterwards if she still wanted to be blessed. She nodded. So I placed my hands on her head and blessed her with a free prayer of blessing. She formulated an intercession for herself and her loved ones. After that, we prayed the Lord's Prayer together and held a moment of silence. It was a solemn moment. Afterwards we had coffee. She was happy about the postcard, felt the blessing and felt strengthened for the everyday life that laid ahead of her.

3 Case study: "It's hell!"

3.1 Meeting

P. is a student of Physical Education, good-looking and smart. He describes himself as gay and lives in a relationship. He also has been suffering from a compulsion to wash for many years, the root cause being that he feels unclean and dirty.

P. was in an inpatient psychiatric ward for several months. Since his discharge, he has been receiving regular outpatient therapeutic treatment. In addition, the therapist had recommended him to work on his destructive image of G*d through receiving pastoral care.

P. comes from a conservative village congregation and participated in an evangelical youth group following his confirmation. His image of G*d is strict, conservative and merciless. The fear of a cruel punishing G*d affected him greatly. He had to deal with it again and again. After his coming out, the situation became even more difficult. He felt ashamed because he was not like the others and felt guilty because he fell in love with other boys from an early age. He felt dirty and sinful and experienced his evangelical circle distance itself from him. They stood by him as a human being, but condemned his actions, which they called sinful and undesirable to G*d. This prevented P. from carrying on the relationship with his partner of several months without a guilty conscience.

P. contacted me via e-mail. I accompanied him for a while. In addition, we wrote numerous emails concerning his judgemental and punitive image of G*d.

The punishing G*d
He described himself being full of self-hatred and having no self-confidence at all. He constantly saw a G*d who was angry with him and disapproved of his life as a gay man. He longed for permission to be the way he felt, and at the same time for an ultimate biblical justification for why his being gay was not sinful or worthy of condemnation.

"In the past, the pastor warned us in my parish. He called homos devil-possessed, shameful creatures. That scared me so much that I prayed day and night. I knew early on that I liked boys. I prayed and prayed, but it didn't help at all. My feelings for men remained. When all that didn't help, I started washing my hands constantly and later my whole body. I felt dirty and defiled, because I had feelings for other guys even as a teenager, even though I didn't dare show any of it, let alone say it or live it."

He experienced himself locked in a hell of damnation and guilt. He moved in a hamster wheel, unable to break out. He had to fulfill his duties, wash his hands constantly, pray and start all over again, even though it didn't help him to break free from his feelings. He didn't get to live his life, unable to see anything positive. He was in hell – the hell that his priest had warned him about and actively pushed him into.

Talking about religious feelings and fears with someone listening
I just listened to him for a long time. He had a strong need to share. He emphasized again and again:

"I can't tell my therapist about my religious feelings. He is an atheist and doesn't understand. But if I don't talk about it, I'll explode. Because I am afraid of G*d and the priest. If I don't talk about it, then I'm missing more than half of the story."

So I listened, showed understanding, encouraged him in a friendly way to keep going, and emphasized several times that I would not pass on anything he told to the therapist or anyone else. This calmed him down. Over time, he became less frantic and began to trust me.

His image of G*d, however, remained that of a strict and omniscient judge who knew full well that P. was sinning.

Idols
I confronted him with the fact that, in my perception, he was holding up an idol and projecting all his fears onto that punitive idol, which had been created by the stern judgemental priest for the purpose of devaluing him and keeping him immature.

This idol kept throwing him back onto the hamster wheel. His obsessive-compulsive disorder also exacerbated the problem. On a rational level, P. could analyze his actions. He understood what I was saying, but it didn't resonate with him at an emotional level. In our next session, at my suggestion, he drew a red card – a stop symbol. He wanted to use that card whenever he was afraid of the punitive and condemning idol, thereby interrupting its power and his own internal entanglement with it. From that point on, he always carried the red card with him. He also drew a green card to go with it – a "Go for it!" card, used for strength and encouragement. He wanted to concentrate on that now.

I encouraged him to live his life and consciously enjoy the time with his partner without feeling guilty.

Positive counter images
In the sessions that followed, we worked on his image of G*d. We searched for and worked on various biblical passages that conveyed very different images of G*d than those he knew. We read the words of Psalms, the creation accounts, and the dialogue between G*d and the prophets. We talked about G*d's presentation of themselves to Moses in the thorn bush: "I am here and I will accompany you out of oppression and slavery!" (Exodus 3). M. particularly liked this assurance. He wrote down some of the Bible passages, which he studied at home. This did him good.

I encouraged him to use this as a basis for another image of G*d and to imagine it again and again. After thinking about it, he adopted the symbol of the cave for himself. He wanted to hide there, but he also wanted to be safe. He wanted to be invisible and at the same time see what was happening. He wanted to dive away and at the same time be saved by an angel of G*d, strengthening him with encouragement, blessing, food and drink. The biblical story of the prophet Elijah, who had experienced G*d in this exact same way, appealed to him. He related Elijah's crises and desert experiences to his life, identified with him, and like Elijah, lamented his suffering to G*d. Finally.

3.2 Queer re-reading of the story of the prophet Elijah
The calling
The story of the prophet Elijah is found in 1 Kings 17 to 2 Kings 2:18. Elijah lived in the 9th century B.C. at the time of Kings Ahab and Ahaziah in the northern kingdom of Israel. Elijah was called by G*d to become a prophet and to proclaim G*d's will:

No other gods, no idolatry, no orgies, no violence. Elijah refused. He felt overwhelmed. But in the end he gave in and proclaimed G*d's word. He wanted to do everything right, and in his over-zealousness, he overshot the mark. Instead of proclaiming G*d's word peacefully, he got involved in a contest with four hundred Baal priests. He won the contest. Completely filled and blinded by his own authority, he murdered the Baal priests with his own hands (1 Kings 18). He had become a religious zealot and extremist who did not shy away from violence. As a result, he was persecuted by the king's soldiers. Elijah fled into the desert, fearing for his life.

In the desert
In the desert, Elijah lay down in a cave and fell asleep, exhausted by the fear of death and the feeling of having failed and being "no better" than his forefathers. He was so frustrated that he no longer wanted to live. In the cave he was twice woken up by an angel. He said to him, "Get up, eat and go!" As if by magic, bread and water were suddenly there. Strengthened by this, Elijah set out on a forty-day march to Mount Horeb, the mountain of G*d.

At Mount Horeb
At Mount Horeb, he again found a cave. There Elijah could finally curse and complain about his fate. G*d heard him and told him to come before him. Elijah was to watch for a sign from G*d. Storms broke out, followed by an earthquake and then a volcanic eruption with fire. But despite these dramatic natural phenomena, G*d remained hidden. Then Elijah heard a "gentle whirring" and sensed G*d in it. Finally, he heard G*d's voice. And amazingly, there was no scolding or lecturing in it. G*d was simply there, just like the angel before. Open, present, gentle. No recommendations, offering neither advice nor strategies for success. Instead, G*d gave Elijah a sober order and spoke forcefully: Travel back through the desert to your everyday life, back to your life! Go and do what you have to do! Not with violence, not with extremist zeal, not with the sword. Approach your circumstances with a sense of proportion, operating within agreed boundaries. There were no threats spoken, but also no reassurances along the lines of "Everything will be all right". The task was simply to return to life.

Elijah's life
And that had been his life until then: Elijah was to die because he had proclaimed unpleasant truths and had gone astray from a spiritual perspective. He had become a murderer. He wanted to shake things up and to challenge the seemingly self-evident existence of people.

In his overzealousness, he had overshot the mark, made enemies, suffered mortal fear and finally did not want to live anymore. But G*d remained with him – in spite of everything, or maybe because of it!

Elijah was a conflicted man. He was not only a believer, but also full of doubt. Not only a daredevil, but also one who had failed, one who had lost his way spiritually and become intoxicated with power. He felt called and incapable at the same time, empowered and helpless, cognizant and misunderstood. In this dichotomy, he fell ill, withdrew, no longer knew what to do.

Queer re-reading
For very different reasons, queer believers are prone to identify with the prophet Elijah. They, too, often feel alone and misunderstood. Some are very devout, but are denied their faith by their congregations or religious groups because as queer people they don't fit the bill. Some used to be overzealous faith warriors themselves and seemed to know exactly what was right and wrong before they came out. They discovered their own internalized homophobia and transphobia and were left feeling insecure. They had neither words nor images for it, shut themselves off, felt lonely and didn't know what to do. Many were thrown off course. Some reacted defiantly and aggressively, others drank too much alcohol or took drugs, while others withdrew from their social environment or suffered from depression. And quite a few ended up alone in some self-made cave and only wanted to be left in peace.

Elijah's experience of being helped by angels who did not judge him was an existential experience for him. This story is encouraging for many queer believers. G*d is there and remains there, regardless of crises, doubts and despair, strengthening and activating the believers' own powers – just as it had encouraged Elijah to stand up and seek his path, in spite of everything.

Elementary care
Basic care finally saved Elijah: food, drink and the order to get up. Nothing more, nothing less. He had to continue walking in the desert, had to expose himself to his demons. The "All is well" was not granted immediately. But forty days later, at Mount Horeb, Elijah met G*d. Not in the storm, not in the thunder, but in the quiet whirring was he able to hear G*d's voice and finally refocus on his own path in life.

He had been completely out of his mind but managed, with G*d's help, to reconnect body, mind, and soul. And G*d stayed with him without making a fuss.

Encouragement
This story encourages many people who, for whatever reason, have lost their way. Even faithful queer people who are struggling to find their place in society can be strengthened by this story. The search for one's sexual orientation and gender identity wears many down. Crises and experiences of exclusion affect many deeply and existentially. But G*d remains and calls out to them: Pay attention to your basic needs: eating, drinking and getting up, just as the angel told Elijah twice. This does not mean recovery and healing will be instantaneous. It is a long process, perhaps a lifelong one. Paths through inner and outer deserts are part of it. And there are no guarantees of recovery. But life goes on. And G*d remains.

3.3 Resonances

"Like Elijah, I also considered suicide once. But I don't want to do that anymore, thank G*d. I feel better, stronger. I can feel myself again for the first time in a long time. But life is still a struggle. And I'm nowhere near where I want to be."

That was P.'s first reaction. And it didn't stop there.

"The story of Elijah shows me that G*d remains. Despite all of life's crises. And it shows me that desert stretches are part of life. They don't just stop. What I want to learn is to hear the voice of G*d in the gentle whirring. I have not paid attention to that until now. I was always so sure that I knew what G*d wanted from me and when He was punishing me, that I never really considered that G*d might be quite different from what I learned from the people in my congregation. I would like to think about this further. The prophet Elijah helps me to finally make room for other images of G*d in my life!"

I encouraged him to continue on this path in small steps. At the same time, I reiterated that he should not stop his therapy under any circumstances. It was absolutely necessary for the treatment of his obsessive-compulsive disorder. Since then, P. has contacted me mainly by e-mail when he has questions about biblical topics. He is on his way. And the story of the prophet Elijah travels with him.

4 Case study: "I don't fit into any pigeonhole!"

4.1 Meeting

I received an e-mail from a person of another regional church. A. was active in a church organization. It had been clear to A. for a long time that A. did not feel like a woman. A. also did not feel trans*, but somewhere in between. Not fitting into any of the pigeonholes, A. was looking for support.

We met online for a first interview. A. told me about the longing to finally be able to live the way A. felt – neither male nor female, but not trans* either. A. wanted to wear their hair shorter, wear different clothes and no longer look at others to see what they thought. Then A. had come across a text of mine on the Internet, which had encouraged A. to contact me. I listened to A. attentively, asked questions, searched with words and understood: no categories, no pigeonholes, no labels. None of these fit!

Talking about yourself as a non-binary person
We arranged regular online counseling sessions and got started. At the beginning, A. talked about their family of origin, school days, socialization. A. told me how things went, what had happened and what was on A.'s mind. And over time, a self-image began to form for A.:

"I see myself as non-binary, neither male nor female. I no longer want to be addressed as a woman, only as a person with my name. This is a makeshift way, but our language is built in a binary way. Black – white, good – evil, young – old, believer – sinner, none of that fits. I am always in between!"

Change of perspective
We worked on the in-between for a long time. Instead of seeing it as a deficit, A. worked out the advantages and strengths it provided: life is full of nuances, there is no clear either/or, but also both and much more. "Diversity instead of simplicity" and other humorous statements helped A. to change their perspective and see the many strengths and resources this offered, instead of the flaws and difficulties.

It did A. good to leave categories and assignments behind and to find other images and words for themselves in a protected space. Nevertheless, A. at the end of a meeting once commented: *"But my colleagues won't think it's funny when I tell them! I'm afraid of that!"*

Finding the words
It took a few more sessions before A. themselves decided to tell some of their close colleagues that A. did not fit within the usual pigeonholes: not-binary, not clear, and no, not trans* either. In preparation, we practiced such conversations in our sessions. Eventually, A. began to tell others about themselves. A. had different experiences and received a lot of understanding. Some were curious, wanted to understand, others reacted defensively and with reservations. A. practiced finding words and learning how to speak about their own situation. It was clear that everyone involved needed time for the dust to settle and to practice using sensitive language, including A. themselves.

Turning point
Being kind to oneself, giving oneself time, not being too impatient, always looking at one's own strengths and resources and not seeing oneself as deficient.

A. found the motto for themselves: *"Trust your own intuition, get out of the pigeonhole and into your life. Live happily in the in-betweens!"*

A. still practices this attitude today. Finally, there was a turning point: A. decided to change jobs in order to be able to act more freely and to be monitored less. A. sent out applications and two months later actually found a new job.

During that time, we studied the biblical story of Joseph and looked for the encouragement in the story, despite all of the conflicts, crises and dangers in life.

4.2 Queer re-reading of Joseph's story

Joseph – Josephine – Jo[11]

Joseph was a quiet and dreamy young man. He made up stories, daydreamed, and stayed close to the tents of his parents Rachel and Jacob. His brothers preferred to romp around and seek adventure. As a teenager, Joseph still had to herd sheep with his brothers. One day the brothers slaughtered an animal, even though their father had forbidden it. Joseph was horrified and told his father about it. In doing so, he invited the anger of the brothers on himself. His father gave him a colorful dress as a thank you gift. Joseph liked to wear his father's skirt and was proud of it. A little later, Joseph had two dreams about first his brothers and then his parents bowing down to him. As a result, his brothers became even more angry with him. A little later, Joseph was called over by his brothers, who were in the field. When he arrived there, they overpowered him and beat him. They stripped him of his skirt and pushed him into a pit. Later they sold the brother for twenty pieces of silver to a merchant passing by with a caravan. After smearing Joseph's skirt with animal blood, they showed it to their father, declaring Joseph dead.

The dress of a princess

In the meantime, several Bible scientists and researchers have found out: The expression used to describe Joseph's skirt in Hebrew ("kethoneth passim") names the dress of a king's daughter, i.e. a princess. The rarely used expression is used e.g. in 2 Samuel 13:18 f. for the dress of the daughter of a king.

Joseph wore the dress of a princess? Impossible! A chosen one of G*d in women's clothes? A hero with feminine features? Unimaginable! This information did not sit well with the male image of many Bible scholars. Nor did it fit Christian tradition, or the image of the believers. It did not fit anyone anywhere. Accordingly, this information was often neglected and omitted.

The strange brother

But where did the brutality, almost frenzy, come from, with which the brothers brutally beat Joseph, humiliated him, tore his dress and threw Joseph into a pit, until they finally sold him? Where had the hatred come from?

The biblical text stresses more than once that Joseph was different: quieter, dreamier, more feminine. Was the envy and jealousy of the brothers perhaps compounded by a fear of the stranger? Did they distance themselves from the brother's otherness? Joseph was not allowed to be as he was: sensitive, full of stories and dreams. The norm for young men dictated something else: physical strength, an adventurous spirit, and an instinct for power.

---

11   First published in: Söderblom (2020a, pp. 53–56).

Joseph – Josephine – Jo

There is a black poet in Philadelphia. His name is J. Mase III, and he describes himself as transgender and queer, beyond binary categories of gender identity and sexual orientation. He has carefully studied the Joseph story in the Bible and has written a poem about it in a creative way. It is called "Joseph – Josephine – Jo." Here is an excerpt from it:

"Joseph / Josephine / Jo … You wore (the skirt) with pride, open, without shame. I am sorry for what happened to you after that. Jo, when your brothers saw you in the flowing dress in all your glory, they got angry. I am so sorry that you were beaten. I am so sorry that you bled, that they tore your dress and smeared it with the red color of your swollen veins".[12]

The dream interpreter

But the betrayal is not the end of the biblical story. Joseph was taken to Egypt and sold to Potiphar, the Pharaoh's Supreme Commander. Joseph worked as a slave there until Potiphar's wife fell in love with him. She made several advances to him, all of which Joseph rejected. Then she accused Joseph of raping her, and Joseph was thrown into prison. In prison, he interpreted the dreams of various people. His interpretations all proved to be correct. Later, when the Pharaoh himself had two dreams that no one in his kingdom understood, he sent for Joseph and told him about the dreams. The first dream was about seven fat cows and seven lean cows. The lean ones ate the fat ones. The second dream was about seven thick and seven thin ears of corn. The thin ones devoured the fat ones.

Joseph interpreted both dreams: after seven good years of harvest in Egypt, seven barren years were to come. Therefore, the Pharaoh should use the good harvest years to stock up for the famine years. Joseph's interpretation was immediately clear to the Pharaoh. He did as Joseph had advised him. Developments over the next years confirmed the dream as well as the interpretation. Joseph was released from prison and became the second in command in Egypt after the Pharaoh. While many neighboring nations suffered from famine, the Egyptians had enough food available thanks to their planned economy. Word spread quickly among the neighboring peoples.

Hello again

It so transpired that Joseph's brothers also came to Egypt. They wanted to buy grain and Joseph was the Pharaoh's negotiator. He recognized his brothers immediately, while they did not recognize him. Only on a second negotiating trip did Joseph reveal himself to them. The brothers were very frightened because they had presumed Joseph dead and now feared his revenge.

---

12 The video used to be available until 2016. Unfortunately, this page no longer exists.

But when Joseph saw his brothers again after all those years, he forgave them, despite all the injustice and suffering he had experienced at their hands. He sent for his father Jacob and the youngest brother, Benjamin, and celebrated a great feast with all of them. Joseph's love was stronger than the hatred of the brothers, his magnanimity greater than their crime. The brothers were unsettled, surprised by Joseph's hospitality and grateful for his generosity. And all of a sudden, they could see Joseph for who he really was – smart, sensitive, successful and different from the others. He had not succeeded with livestock, but with listening, dream interpretation and his intuition. He was neither better nor worse than the others, but different. Maybe he was just more sensitive. Today he would maybe call himself trans*, probably rejecting any categorization. What is certain, though, is that he survived the tragic combination of betrayal, loss of home, and exile. In the foreign land he was able to build a new life. And all this time Joseph had not forgotten the G*d of his fathers – a G*d who was with him and protected him.

Joseph – Josephine – Jo II
The poet J. Mase III related Joseph's story to his own life and interpreted the end of the biblical story like follows:

"Joseph / Josephine / Jo ... Your love has penetrated the darkness of reservations and broke it. And for the first time your family saw you as you are, so wonderful. Because it was you who saved the people from hunger.

Dear Joseph of Genesis, Josephine, Jo ..., I claim your story for every gay, lesbian, queer child who is told it is unholy; for every gay, lesbian, queer person who is told: If you want to live, you must let your faith die."[13]

Joseph's story is encouraging for those who identify with those on the margins. For the reserved, the shy, the emotional, for those who feel different, who are in search of themselves, of their sexual orientation, of their gender identity. To all of them this story shows that brutal violence does not have the last word! There is a safe place with G*d, for Joseph, Josephine, and for Jo.

4.3 Resonances
A. was fascinated by the story, but at first we sat in silence. We read the story again, talked about individual paragraphs, exchanged ideas about the poet J. Mase III's vivid interpretation. A. was impressed that J. Mase III allowed himself to connect the story of Joseph to his life. The lines in the poem helped A. to relate the story to their own life as well. For a long time A. had not been able to do that. The internalized law they had

---
13 See footnote 12.

picked up from their congregation that the words in the Bible were G*d's word and had nothing to do with their own life, ran too deep.

To do otherwise was to contaminate the stories and commit blasphemy. When I asked how this could happen, A. could not answer me and remained silent.

After a while I added:

"Biblical stories keep linking the earlier experiences of the people of the nation of Israel to events in later centuries. G*d also establishes these references in biblical self-imagery time and again. G*d reveals themselves to Moses at the thorn bush and explains to him that G*d has already been on the journey with Abraham and Sarah, Isaac and Rebekah, Jacob and Rachel and has blessed them. Later, G*d gives Moses the Decalogue tablets at Mount Sinai, reminding Moses and the people of Israel that it was G*d who had led them out of Egypt. The remaining prophetic speeches also refer to the primal experiences of the people of Israel with their G*d. These are referred to again and again. In this way, life stories and earlier stories of faith are already intertextually related to each other in the Bible. When believers relate biblical stories to their lives today, this is the same process."

A. nodded and let what they had heard sink in. Then we continued to share the biblical story. At the end of the meeting, A. summarized everything that had been said:

"I am encouraged by the story. Joseph was different, did not fit in, did not fulfill the expectations everybody had of him. He attracted hatred and envy, had to endure violence, restrictions, and prison. But finally he found his place and did what he was good at. And G*d stayed with him and blessed him. Just as G*d blesses me. Just as I am. That feels good!"

5 Case study: "What is normal, actually?"

5.1 Meeting

We met at the entrance of the botanical garden. We knew each other from previous ESG events. Z. was studying architecture.

Z. greeted me with a smile, thanked me for coming, and off we went. After a few minutes of silence, he began:

"Well, I wanted to talk to you because I thought of you right away. My pals just laugh at me and don't take me seriously. It's not easy ..."

I nodded encouragingly and smiled at him.

He continued, "All right, I'll give it a try: I fall in love with lesbian or bisexual women all the time. And even when we've been dating for a while, eventually she leaves me for a woman. Recently, this happened to me again. That's not normal, is it?"

Normal

For a while we talked about what was "normal" anyway, while going about our walk slowly. The fresh air was doing us both good, as was facing the same direction together.

Questioning the construct of "normal" helped us to bond with each other. We laughed as we told each other what we thought was "not normal". There was quite a lot. Eventually, I asked more questions.

Z. told me about his type of women and his experiences. Somehow, she always left him for another woman or it didn't work out in the first place, because she was more interested in women. By now he had become very hesitant to go on a date with women, he explained to me. He was sure: If he was interested in them, they would turn out to be lesbians.

Personal reaction

I nodded and remained silent. We continued walking side by side, casually watching two blackbirds sitting on a bush who seemed to be teasing each other. Then I told him about my experiences as a student, when I had fallen in love with heterosexual women more than once. These experiences had been quite painful for me, because nothing had ever come of it: the women had been friends of mine or not, but friendship was all they were ever interested in. What followed was a loose conversation about types of women and our shared experience of not progressing to dating level with past romantic interests. While the reasons for that had been different, what united us was the shared sense of disappointment Z. became more lively and continued to talk.

Showing pain

I was able to feel his pain behind the casual and somewhat cynical facade for the first time at this point, and told him so. He nodded and welled up. For a while we said nothing and just kept walking side by side. It was okay to show pain.

Shelter

After a while, I continued to talk about myself and shared my thoughts on why I had fallen in love only with heterosexual women for a long time. I felt that I had not been ready for a relationship at that time. Sure, I was sad and frustrated that my feelings of falling in love had not been reciprocated, but at that time that had also protected me. As long as I only fell in love with women I couldn't have, I didn't have to invest anything or show myself, and I certainly did not have to get involved in a relationship. At the time, that had obviously been the best solution for me. Anything else would have been too soon. I had needed time to be ready for a relationship. This had a lot to do with my coming out, my view of myself, and my low self-esteem at the time. I told Z. about it quite openly. Z. turned to me, was surprised and obviously grateful for my words.

"I wouldn't have guessed that you used to have trouble with relationships, too. That surprises me. But it honestly also relieves me a little and takes pressure off my shoulders!" he said thoughtfully.

Benefit
I nodded to him. Finally, I asked him if there could be any advantage in the fact that he had often fallen in love with women who were not available. Could there also be a benefit in that? Z.'s answer came quickly: Absolutely! He was independent and actually liked living alone. The most important thing for him was a sense of community, which he experienced in his shared apartment, within his study group, and in his prayer group. He fell silent. After a while, he nodded. There was something to the idea that maybe he didn't really want to open himself up to a relationship. He'd have to think about that some more, he said. But what should he do about the fact that he was obviously more attracted to tomboyish women?

Change of view
After he had explained to me that tomboyish to him meant sporty, practical, and nature-loving, we came up with places where he could meet "tomboyish women" like that – at sports, hiking or climbing tours, or at Eco camps. He started laughing as we continued collecting locations. By now we had completed three circuits of the botanical gardens and the allotted hour was up. He smiled and emphasized that it was doing him good to be understood by someone who did not dismiss him as eccentric or crazy.

"Being taken seriously and being recognized for who I am – that is the most important thing to me!" he said. I confirmed that and told him that it was probably the most important thing for all of us, and certainly for me. Z. also wanted to see if he could join a student hiking trip and winked at me. I winked back.

We agreed to stay in touch via WhatsApp and I told him that he was welcome to call or e-mail me if he needed to talk further. We have been in touch ever since.

What does normal mean?
Not feeling normal also works the other way around. If you feel heterosexual yourself but fall in love with LGBTQI+ people, it's obviously not easy either. Z. was laughed at for falling in love with lesbians; as a result, he didn't dare to tell more people about his situation. The lesbian pastor was just the right person to open up to about his pain and suffering. He trusted me to take him seriously. In me, he saw a role model in living self-acceptance, and assumed accordingly that I would not react to others in a derogatory or dismissive manner.

Finally able to talk about it
We discovered similar tastes in women and got to talk about it. The walk through the park also contributed to Z. loosening up and finally being able to open up about his problem. He didn't find my experiences as a young female student embarrassing, but

wanted to hear more about them. My personal response to his pain helped him take his own pain seriously and not brush it off. My question about what could be gained from unrequited infatuation also got him thinking. Z. wanted to explore the question further, about whether he had perhaps unconsciously taken precautions to prevent someone getting too close to him, or whether he simply had to look in other places to search for his type of woman.

"I thought it was great that you talked to me about these things. That way, I was also able to sometimes laugh and rant or rave about other women. Like you, too. That was cool! You helped me change my perspective on that. I think it's amazing how important a lesbian pastor can be to me as a heterosexual man. Thank you!"

We said our goodbyes at the exit of the botanical gardens and Z. went his way, whistling.

In another meeting at the ESG, we talked about the double commandment of love, which I had previously preached on in a devotion.

5.2 Queer re-reading of the double commandment of love

Connoisseur of the Hebrew Bible

Jesus was a Jew and knew the Torah and the Hebrew Scriptures. He had learned them early on in the temple. On the one hand, it was clear to him that not one iota of the law could be changed (Matthew 5:18). On the other hand, he interpreted the laws in an undogmatic, everyday and people-friendly way. "The law is for human beings, not human beings for the law" (Mark 2:27), Jesus said clearly, when he was approached by scholars. He had just helped and healed a person on Shabbat.

The highest bid

When asked by others what the highest law was, Jesus answered without hesitation:
"The highest commandment is this:
Listen, Israel,
the Lord our G*d is the Lord alone,
and you shall love the Lord your G*d with all your heart, with all your soul,
with all your mind and with all your strength" (Deuteronomy 6:4–5).
The other is:
"You shall love your neighbor as yourself" (Leviticus 19:18).
"There is no other commandment greater than these" (Mark 12:29–31, Matthew 22:37–39).

If you take a closer look at these sentences, you will see that Jesus did not invent the double commandment of love. He merely quoted the words from the Hebrew Bible. However, it was Jesus that linked the two commandments and related them to each other.

Love of G*d, love of neighbor, love of self: for Jesus, this love triad was interconnected. One resulted from the other. Whoever loved G*d, he was convinced, would also respect his fellow human beings. And the person who did so would also take care of himself or herself. In this respect, the double commandment of love is actually a triple commandment. Self-love is often forgotten when it comes to the interpretation of the text. However, it stands on an equal footing with the other two love commandments in the text.

And what is also important to stress is that this tripartite love commandment is not about romantic feelings of love; it is about respect, self-esteem and recognition. These are the ingredients that were just as important for Judaism at that time, as they were for the peaceful coexistence of believers in that society. These are still key ingredients today.

Words and deeds
Jesus also emphasized that this double commandment sums up all the other commandments and therefore serves as the highest commandment. He adhered to this throughout his life – even if he reacted critically to the interpretation of other commandments. He also adhered to it himself. He prayed to G*d, preached G*d's word, and acted accordingly. He visited the ordinary people, listened to them, ate and drank with them, laughed, prayed and celebrated with them. He took them from the margins to the center, he recognized them and gave them back their dignity. That is true charity! And that is what it is still about today: giving people back their dignity, no matter whether they are rich or poor, male, female or diverse, healthy or sick, young or old, homo- or heterosexual, black, white or persons of color … Because they are all children of G*d and created in G*d's image. This is the central message of Jesus!

And that is why it is so important to examine one's own attitudes and actions. Am I directed by prejudices and stereotypes? Do they shape my behavior towards people I don't know and who are foreign to me?

Self-care
The other message is just as important, though: Am I taking good care of myself? Do I respect myself? Do I accept myself as who I am? For only those who love themselves likewise are able to love G*d and neighbor. Otherwise, the whole system becomes unbalanced or leads to a martyr complex.

Many queer believers are no strangers to this. They struggle to love G*d and their neighbor, but cannot love themselves. Shame and feelings of inferiority run too deep. Internalized homophobia and transphobia keep them from accepting themselves. And not only queer people are familiar with this feeling.

Many who, for whatever reason, feel different or held back also struggle with self-esteem and self-respect. The command to love G*d and your neighbor as yourself is particularly relevant to these people.

Don't forget yourself in the process of loving G*d and others!

5.3 Resonances

Self-love

Z. knew the double commandment of love and it was important to him. At the same time, he admitted that he had never been that aware of the self-love concept. So far, his life had always been about love of G*d and love of neighbor. Self-love had somehow fallen by the wayside. It simply had not played a big role in his life until now. Perhaps that also rang true in his social circles. He wanted to think about that more. But he understood that this could have consequences.

"If I don't take good care of myself, no one will," he said thoughtfully. *"If I show my feelings to my buddies, I get laughed at or thought of as a wimp. I mean, that's crap. So what do I learn from that? I don't show my feelings to everyone anymore and I'm more careful about who I talk to about certain things. That's pure self-protection and that is also about self-love."*

Concepts of normality

I nodded. Then we focused on the concept of normality again and explored its positive and negative connotations. Z. himself considered the fact that he fell in love with lesbians as abnormal. But what does that mean? Were the women-loving women also abnormal? And who actually determines what is normal? And what are the implications of this?

"Not being normal is always devalued and seen negatively," Z. said. *"That's already the root evil. Because if you can't see yourself as normal, it may also be difficult to develop self-confidence."*

I confirmed this to him and emphasized that I had heard this type of self-devaluation from many queer people, but also from people like him.

Z. looked at me. He had obviously made a connection. We agreed on doing some exercises at our next meetings. He wanted to make a more conscious attempt to take care of himself and no longer be ashamed of his feelings. The "Threefold Commandment of Love," as Z. now called it, would help him.

UNDERSTANDING

IV First findings

1 Framework: Safe places and reliable time frames

"Is this conversation really confidential? Will everything stay between us?"(J.). These were J.'s first questions and in that way, the conversation with J. wasn't any different to those of other students with a pastoral care concern. The safe conversational framework guarantees a protective space for all involved parties, which is indispensable. This is particularly true when queer students like J. seek counsel with me. For them, the safe space is extremely important: on the one hand, they sometimes share thoughts and feelings with me that only their very best friends know about. On the other hand, quite a few are afraid of negative reactions from family members and their social circles, when it comes to them being queer. Pastoral confidentiality and concern for the safety of those seeking pastoral care is therefore a basic prerequisite for queer-affirming pastoral care. A safe place also involves a clear and reliable framework: it needs time free of the hustle and bustle of everyday life and a clear time frame. A hospitable space, a cup of coffee, tea or water won't hurt, either. These prerequisites create a sense of security and freedom in the counseling room.

2 Attitude: Appreciation and respect

"It feels so good to not have to explain and justify myself. I know that I will be taken seriously, just as I am!" (J.).

This sentiment that J. expressed following our meeting is one that I encounter quite often, regardless of the age of those seeking pastoral care, because even queer students, despite their relative youth, have experienced trauma, insults, and exclusion. Some of them have been singled out, whispered about and laughed at. Others were bullied in their youth groups, teased and insulted by the other children because they were somehow different. They were not boys; they were not girls – they themselves lacked the words for exactly who they were. They didn't fit into any of the pigeonholes and didn't enjoy the usual opposite sex relations that their peers engaged in. That made them outcasts. Others come to me because they don't feel at home in their own bodies. Some are considering gender reassignment. Others simply don't want to be pigeonholed, as A. had told me, while quite a few come from religious homes and are afraid to tell their parents about their true selves.

It does not matter who comes to me – I look forward to meeting young and older people regardless of who they are, where they come from, how they live and love, or what their gender identity is. I see them as children of G*d, wonderfully created in G*d's image, loved and blessed in their uniqueness and dignity.

They feel the appreciation and respect I show them and many are grateful that with me, they don't have to explain or justify themselves, they don't have to fear a moral lecture or a theological sermon on sin. Of course, heterosexual students also come to counseling sessions, like Z., appreciating being respected for who they are. All people need recognition, also and especially in pastoral care.

For me it is frightening to see how many young people have already experienced devaluation in the family circle, at school, in sports clubs or at a church youth group. Queer-affirming pastoral care shows: *"You are wonderfully made, just as you are!"* (according to Psalm 139:14). Acceptance and recognition are foundational to pastoral care work – out of conviction and not from a sense of duty.

3 Knowledge: Knowing about minority stress

"You know, pastor, I'm sometimes afraid of being offended again, like I was in my congregation" (P.).

When a chaplain knows the trauma, insults, and arrogance that some of us have had to endure due to our sexual orientation or gender identity, relief is the result. Just being able to say: "You understand this, don't you?", is an enormous relief.

Physical, emotional and religious minority stress cuts to the very core of who we are. "Religiously authorized" language that demonizes and threatens people with hell and damnation, as experienced by P., for example, hurts those affected deeply, leaving them shaken. This is especially true for those who come from very pious homes and backgrounds. Conversion therapies legitimized by religion can also have traumatic effects.

Preaching about hell with threats of damnation often have toxic long-term effects that can damage young people's self-esteem for years or even decades to come. Queer-affirming counselors are aware of the multi-layered consequences of minority stress and incorporate them into their counseling work.

A confidential narrative does not become a confession, but can bring about reassurance and resilience. Counseling can create a protected space to share stress, pressure and hurt feelings. And if these feelings are taken seriously and dealt with, they can even become spaces of freedom in which pastoral care seekers can try out various options and see which work. Other resources can be discovered and built on. Biblical stories, prayers and rituals can help to give expression to situations and to reinterpret them in a positive light. An appreciation of how theological language works, and a knowledge of queer-theological re-readings of biblical texts are important and helpful for this.

The minority stress model

The minority stress model was developed by Ilan H. Meyer, a lecturer at the Williams Institute of the UCLA School of Law in Los Angeles in the 1990s (cf. Meyer 1995). The model states that minorities and members of stigmatized groups face increased (structural and institutional) stressors due to their minority position. This stress is multi-faceted and can be experienced physically, emotionally, and religiously/spiritually. Moreover, it is not just situational stress, but involves stressors that plague many affected individuals throughout their lives. In this way, minority stress leading to anxiety can become chronic and limit the quality of life enormously. For LGBTQI+ persons, it can lead to toxic self-hatred and/or internalized bi/trans/homophobia, and even severe depression.

Examples of physical stress

Affected persons are threatened or exposed to physical violence; they experience body shaming, teasing and insults because their appearance is allegedly not masculine or feminine enough. They experience pressure to conform in terms of posture, charisma, sex appeal, hairstyles, makeup, hair or facial hair and clothing. Same-sex sexuality is forbidden, criminalized, and pathologized by uttering threats of violence as a punishment. All of these threats serve to lock those affected into heteronormative and binary behavioral systems.

Examples of psychological/emotional stress

People are implicitly or explicitly forbidden same-sex feelings of infatuation and desire. They feel the pressure to conform in terms of male and female role allocations and behaviors. If they do not conform, they are threatened with, at a minimum, the withdrawal of attention and recognition, participating and belonging in family systems/peer groups and the community.

Examples of spiritual/religious stress

The assertion that same-sex love and sexuality are not desired by G*d, but are sinful and come from the devil, often leads to acts of spiritual violence (cf. Schneider 2021).[14] The same applies to the threat of withdrawal of love, and threats of hell and damnation. Such phrases are uttered primarily by right-wing evangelical and fundamentalist groups of all denominations and confessions. They are used specifically as leverage to force a confession of thoughts or actions that are considered deviant or condemnable. Exclusion from religious groups, church services, communion or Eucharistic celebrations, or from other church activities are further threats. A substantial number of believers have been offered alternative "treatment approaches", ranging from (demonic) exorcism to religiously legitimized conversion therapies[15], which can have extremely traumatic consequences for those affected. People with experiences of spiritual violence are therefore particularly dependent on pastoral care being offered in a queer-affirming manner, to prevent re-traumatization.

4 Evaluation: Change of perspective and expansion of action

"I never thought of it that way!" (A.).

In almost all counseling conversations in a queer context, I sense my clients feeling inferior, deficient in some way, or 'stained' at some point. Being queer is experienced as a stigma. The experience mirrors the beliefs of people in the wider community and/or within the religious peer group. Instead of recognizing these beliefs as structural issues, though, these attributions and stereotypes are internalized and perceived as personal shortcomings. This was the case for M., who, due to coming out late in life, felt that she was neither normal within the heterosexual nor in the queer world. A. described the situation like standing between chairs, as the binary world surrounding A. was simply not a fit for them. This experience was also shared by students J. and P., even though the

---

14 In her autobiographical book, Hilde Raastad (2022) powerfully describes forms of spiritual violence she suffered as a lesbian and theologian.

15 Conversion therapies give the erroneous impression that homosexuality is "curable" and can be corrected to an asexual or heterosexual behavior, for example by light or electroshock therapies. However, there is no scientific evidence supporting this. The Hirschfeld-Eddy Foundation (2020) estimates the number of affected persons in Germany at one to two thousand. For this reason, the "Law for Protection against Conversion Treatments" (KonvBG; Federal Ministry of Justice 2020) was enacted in Germany in June 2020. It protects minors up to the age of 18. It also offers protection to adults who have not given explicit consent to such therapies.

university environment is supposed to offer a far greater degree of personal individual freedom.

Reframing and being open to further new perspectives takes time in pastoral care and counseling work. In most cases however, there is further work to be done beyond a change of perspective and discovering new strengths.

In a religious context, this process is primarily about addressing evaluations of the queer person that have mostly negative connotations, in terms of sexual orientation and gender identities, and which link to concepts of sin and remoteness from G*d. P.'s struggle against concepts of a punishing and judging G*d and against priestly statements of being damned to hell serve as a dramatic expression of this spiral of devaluation. But other people seeking advice also wrestled with internalized devaluation and low self-esteem, as was especially evident in the case of M. and Z.

Careful steps are needed to challenge outdated evaluations and norms and to change perspectives. However, such steps are only sustainable if practiced repeatedly over a long period of time. Those who change their views and broaden their perspectives also learn to expand their own scope for action and eventual stop seeing themselves as victims of other people's attitudes and prejudices. The options that arise can then be explored and tested out together in the safety of a counseling session.

5 Challenge: "Clobber Passages"

"But it's written in the Bible that it's sinful and not Godly. What am I supposed to tell the people at my church?" (J.).

For queer-affirming pastoral care, it is not necessary to know all the Bible verses that judge homosexuality negatively. However, it is important to make clear that these texts are over two thousand years old and that they were written at a completely different time and in cultural and religious contexts that are not applicable to our life today. Therefore, they cannot be used literally as moral guidance and instructions for action in the 21st century.

Nevertheless, it is useful to know the "Clobber Passages", especially when dealing with students from environments that take the Bible literally. I will therefore give a small overview of the texts and what can be said about them in the context of pastoral care in Chapter V.

It is important to point out that 21st century scientific knowledge around sexual orientation and gender identities cannot be compared with knowledge from the first century A. D., or from centuries B. C. Therefore, individual biblical verses cannot be used as moral guidelines for the 21st century.

6 Workshop: Queer re-readings of Biblical texts

The overall message of the Bible is one of encouragement and liberation. This message can be expressed in queer-affirming counseling conversations in simple words suitable for everyday life, if that is what is desired.

Stories of life and faith

What a queer re-reading of biblical texts has shown in all of the case studies so far, is that it enabled those seeking pastoral care to relate their life stories to a biblical story, creating resonance in the interpretive space. It helped them to realize that the Bible is full of stories of people who were confronted with questions of faith, doubts, crises and injustices in the face of their G*d and had to learn to deal with them. What also helped them was to discover that G*d stayed alongside people and did not reject them, even though they struggled with G*d and their fate – for example, Jacob, Joseph or Elijah. In other stories, the protagonists had to deal with fundamental changes – for example, those who had lived with Jesus and had to process his death and resurrection. Pastoral care seekers experienced that queer life stories can be related to biblical stories and that queer people play an important role as actors in an interpretative workshop. They felt that their life stories were relevant and that biblical stories could also be empowering for their lives. For people who keep hearing that being queer and Christian don't go together, these serve as a source of encouragement.

Creative energy

Relating biblical and everyday stories to one another released creative energy in those seeking pastoral care. The undogmatic engagement with biblical texts, which allowed subjective references and associations to be made, instead of condemning the hearer, had a liberating effect on them. Instead of being objects of theological doctrines and moral devaluation, they became subjects in conversation, subjects of their own story. In this respect, it is helpful to be aware of queer approaches to biblical texts, or at least to be open to allowing personal references to be applied to biblical texts. In this way, biblical texts can be both encouraging and liberating.

7 Reflection: The role of pastoral caregivers

Street Credibility

In all of the counseling sessions described above, it was important to those seeking counsel that they came to me in my capacity as an openly lesbian counselor. As a queer pastor, I have a certain "street credibility", i.e. an everyday credibility that leads to a certain amount of trust being placed in me prior to the conversations. This has the advantage that the threshold for requesting pastoral care from a queer person and opening up to this person is lower. However, it may also be the case that a queer pastor cannot automatically fulfill all expectations, is not a better pastor, and is not suitable for all individuals and all presented issues. The disappointment can be double when queer pastors do not live up to expectations.

Empathy can be both an opportunity and a challenge. Queer pastors are probably familiar with many of the problems and conflicts on which people seek advice. Empathy and understanding of the situation are therefore easier to come by. However, strong empathy can also lead to queer pastors lacking the distance required to provide professional pastoral care. They may also be triggered by their own traumatic experiences, which may impact on their ability to act appropriately. They therefore tread a fine line between closeness and distance, empathy and professional distance, knowledge and openness to new ideas, and all while keeping an eye on the care seeker's experience.

For these reasons, there are various advantages and disadvantages to different pastors offering queer-affirming pastoral care. As long as the respective challenges are reflected upon and one's own role and position questioned, it is possible for all pastors to offer queer-affirming pastoral care. This also applies to other life events; not all pastors need to have shared similar experiences in order to offer professional pastoral care in these areas.

Queer-affirming communication

In the case studies, pastoral care seekers all referred to the queer-friendly statements of the Evangelische Studierendengemeinde (Protestant University Chaplaincy) on its website and in social media. Some explicitly mentioned queer-friendly events and projects of the ESG that they had attended previously. This clearly shows that pastors do not have to be queer in order to offer queer-affirming pastoral care. What they need to make transparent, however, is that they are working from a queer-affirming perspective. Furthermore, they must be aware of the following phenomenon:

Many queer people are distrustful or even defensive when it comes to offers from church facilities and institutions. Too many of them have already experienced exclusion, devaluation or worse in a church environment. They might also be skeptical, fearing forms of "pink washing."[16] Therefore, none of them

---

16 In cases of pink washing, the apparent support of the LGBTQI+ is utilized to appear modern and progressive or to recruit new target groups for offers and products. However, this is done without a clear and transparent position in terms of content or consequences for action.

will go to a counseling session "on a whim". Most will inquire very carefully in advance on what to expect. If there is even the slightest suspicion that a pastor might have an ambivalent or even negative relationship to queer people, they will not come.

Queer-friendly setting

Being queer *and* being Christian encompasses a complex and ambivalent experiential mixture that includes experiences of humiliation, exclusion and religiously legitimized devaluation. In this respect, it is important that a queer-affirming pastoral care setting is guaranteed and also publicly communicated. This is what this might look like: This place is a safe place for queer people. It is welcoming, inclusive and queer-friendly. It is crucial that this place not only states this on its website, but also demonstrates it through queer-friendly projects, thereby living up to its statement. If, in addition, a queer-affirming mission statement exists and rainbow flags, flyers and posters indicate that the place is queer-friendly, then queer people will come, help shape the space and, if necessary, also ask for pastoral care.

V Dealing with "Clobber Passages"

1 Challenge

"Clobber Passages" are passages in the Bible that contain statements against homo sexuality. They include: Genesis 19:1–13; Leviticus 18:22; Leviticus 20:13; Romans 1:18–32; 1 Corinthians 6:9f.; 1 Timothy 1:9–10.

As a rule, these verses are quoted literally from the Bible without being located within the historical, cultural and socio-political context of the time in which they were written. In this way, these few verses are uncritically misused to biblically substantiate derogatory attitudes towards homosexuality and to mark it as an inviolable judgement of G*d, with the aim of staving off any counter-arguments. The problem with this approach, is that new, often more scientific biblical hermeneutics, are undermined or completely ignored.

Quoting single verses out of context creates moral condemnation. This can be seen in statements such as:

*"But the Bible says…", "G*d abhors homosexuality!"* and *"It is sinful and not wanted by G*d!"* Such utterances are used as brutal weapons against people who can barely defend themselves, and creating the illusion that they cannot be opposed.

"G*d condemns homosexuality!" It is all too easy to say such things; these people claim to know G*d so well that they feel entitled to fire out these sentences (in both terms of the word) like a loaded weapon, sending bullets into the hearts of the objects of their judgement. After all, that's what the Bible says, isn't it?

This is in stark contrast to historical criticism in the field of biblical hermeneutics recognized among biblical scholars for over a hundred years and still practiced today. Such historical criticism focuses on the temporal, geographical, cultural, religious and linguistic contextualization of Bible verses and entire biblical books. It also distances itself historically from the interpretation of texts. That is to say, biblical texts cannot provide any information regarding sexuality, forms of cohabitation and the challenges of diverse gender identities of the 21st century, since these modern forms of relationships and identities were unknown at that time.

Nevertheless, in terms of content and morality, the "Clobber Passages" still wield an enormously high authority in many Christian groups and congregations and have a concrete impact on individual and collective attitudes and positions on LGBTQI+ issues. For this reason, it is important for queer-affirming pastoral care to offer a thorough theological and contextual explanation of these well-known passages. Those who simply claim that G*d loves everyone equally, disregard the religious distress that many pastoral care seekers carry with them with regard to the misapplication of literal passages from Scripture. This distress must be taken seriously and the reason for the pain (namely, misappropriation of Scripture) substantially challenged and invalidated. To achieve this, some biblical groundwork is important, which I will summarize below.[17]

2 Theological Classification and Explanation of the Clobber Passages

Genesis 19:1–13[18]

1 The two angels came to Sodom in the evening. Lot was sitting in the gate of Sodom. When he saw them, he arose, approached them, threw himself face down to the ground 2 and said, "Please, my lords, stop at your servant's house, stay overnight and wash your feet. In the morning you can continue on your way." No, they said, we want to spend the night in the square. 3 He pressed them so hard that they stopped at his house and entered it.

He prepared a meal for them, had unleavened bread made, and they ate. 4 They had not yet gone to sleep when the men of the city surrounded the house, the men of

---

17 Cf. Plisch (2016); Lings (2013) for these remarks as a whole.
18 Cf. Lings (2013, pp. 241–281). For an in-depth religious study, see Brinkschröder (2006).

Sodom, young and old, all the people from far and wide. 5 They called for Lot and asked him, "Where are the men who came to you tonight? Bring them out to us, we will deal with them. 6 Then Lot went out to them at the door, and shut it behind him, 7 and said, My brethren, do not evil. 8 Look, I have two daughters who have not yet consorted with a man. I will bring them out to you. Then do to them as you please. Only do nothing to these men, for that is why they have come under the protection of my roof.

9 And they said, "Go away". And they said, "Someone is coming, a stranger, and he wants to be a judge. Now we want to do more evil to you than to them." So they put the man, Lot, to the sword, and were about to break open the door. 10 Then those men stretched out their hand, pulled Lot into the house and locked the door. 11 Then they struck the men outside the house, great and small, with blindness, so that they tried in vain to find the entrance. 12 The men said to Lot, "Who else belongs to you here? A son-in-law, sons, daughters, or anyone else in the city? Take them away from this place! 13 We will destroy this place, for great is the lamentation that has come upon them to G*d. G*d has sent us to destroy the city."

Biased interpretations of the biblical story of Sodom and Gomorrah are still used today to slander and condemn queer people worldwide. Yet the story is about something very different.

What the text says

What the text in Genesis 19:1–13 tells us first of all is this:

Two angels visited Lot in the city of Sodom. Lot invited the two strangers, gave them food and drink, and granted them hospitality and lodging. All the men of Sodom, young and old, had heard that two strangers had come to Lot's house. They came to the house and circled it. They shouted at Lot to surrender the two strangers so they could rape them.

Lot tried to appease the men and offered them his two daughters, both of whom were still virgins. He wanted to protect the right of hospitality against the strangers and was willing to hand over his two daughters to the wild mob in return. In his patriarchal logic, the strangers counted more than the women. The mob, however, did not calm down and continued to demand the surrender of the two strangers. Then the two stepped out of the door and struck the men with blindness and drove them away. They then asked for Lot's family members. For all the others were to be destroyed as punishment.

Who was it?

To recap all the men from the city of Sodom had gathered in front of Lot's house. Is it possible that every man living in Sodom was gay? Most certainly not. A number of studies estimate that the percentage of same-sex lovers in most cultures makes up for 3 to 10 percent of the population. Using this statistic as a guide, it seems highly unlikely that more than 10 percent of the men from Sodom were homosexual. Or in other words: 90 to 97 percent of the men at Lot's door were most probably heterosexual. Why then was the "sin of Sodom" related exclusively to homosexual men? Bias and prejudice have made this interpretation possible, etching it into the collective memory through the centuries.

The view from the prophet Ezekiel

The biblical book of the prophet Ezekiel recorded why G*d's wrath was directed at Sodom:

"This was the sin of Sodom. They were proud, had too much to eat and were wealthy. But they did not help the poor and needy. They were haughty and did detestable things in my sight. Therefore, when I saw them, I removed them" (Ezekiel 16:49–50).

The prophet Ezekiel clearly emphasized that an excess of pride as well as an abundance of possessions and wealth led to the downfall of Sodom. For the Sodomites would share nothing with the poor and needy, and they practiced heinous violence against strangers, women and those in need of shelter. It was about the fundamental violation of the right to hospitality, about threatening sexual violence towards strangers and Lot's daughters. What the story was definitely not about was homosexuality!

Xenophobic and misogynistic environment

Lot did defend the right to hospitality on the strangers' behalf. But the real scandal of the story is that he would have sacrificed his daughters to the wild mob to keep it quiet. He would have tolerated sexual violence towards his daughters.

The whole setting portrays a xenophobic and misogynistic environment with strictly patriarchal and heteronormative power relations. Sexual violence towards strangers, women and those in need of shelter was obviously part of male-dominated everyday life in the cities of Sodom and Gomorrah.

Queer perspective

From a queer perspective, it becomes clear that queer people would have been just as unwelcome in this city as strangers and those in need of shelter and protection. The story has been misused for centuries to condemn gay men, even though it was not about them at all. In addition, the story portrays a xenophobic, misogynistic, and queerphobic environment, which would not be safe for vulnerable people even today. The "sin of Sodom" is therefore not one of homosexuality, but a violation of hospitality and the threat of sexual violence.

Appropriation of divine power

Another interpretation says that the men of Sodom suspected that the strangers were messengers of G*d. By subjecting them to sexual acts, they sought to obtain divine power, authority and influence (cf. Lings 2013, p. 281).

The exercise of excessive physical power and religious rhetoric coupled with sexual violence was, and still is, a lamentable feature of military warfare. It speaks to a lack of moderation and the acquisition of power. This willingness to resort to sexual violence, no matter who the victim was, was the "Sin of Sodom", committed by all the men of Sodom.

Effects of misinterpretation

Throughout the history of Christian tradition, the story of Sodom and Gomorrah has been cited as one of the most powerful arguments against homosexuality. The text became the proof par excellence that G*d hates gay men. The proverbial negative connotations of the term "Sodomites" have led to a perpetuation of the misinterpretation of this Scripture, which has brought endless suffering to gay men and other queer people. It shows what disastrous effects the deliberate misinterpretation of biblical verses has brought about throughout the centuries. It has led to slander and ostracism, even murder and burning at the stake.

The story of Sodom and Gomorrah has been instrumental in legitimizing Christian persecution and condemnation of gay men. It is time to clarify the misinterpretation once and for all and never again use this text as a weapon against innocent people.

Leviticus 18:22 and 20:13[19]
18:22 You must not sleep with a man as one sleeps with a woman; that would be an abomination.

20:13 If one sleeps with a man as one sleeps with a woman, they have committed an abomination; both of them deserve death; their blood is on themselves.

The Book of Leviticus, or the 3rd Book of Moses, is not a biblical history book, but a collection of laws and instructions on how the people of Israel were to behave. The collection was intended primarily for the priests (Leviticus 1:1). The laws were intended to give direction and guidance to the monotheistic community of Israel as they journeyed through polytheistic nations. The laws set the Hebrew people apart religiously and culturally from their neighbors (Leviticus 20:22–24). In this respect, the laws defined new ways of worshipping G*d, cre-

---

19 Cf. Lings (2013, pp. 195–238).

ated a common approach to just coexistence, and covered all aspects of life in community. It was predominantly about purity commandments.

The two biblical quotes come from the so-called Holiness Law (Leviticus 17–26). These chapters deal specifically with how Israel had to behave in dealing with G*d and how each and every individual could attain purity before G*d.

It covered dietary regulations, dress codes, prohibition of cult prostitution and idolatry, and the handling of sacrificial animals. Wearing mixed fabrics was forbidden, as was mixing and eating different foods.

The list of acts considered lewd and worthy of death is long: idolatry, divination, child sacrifice, inbreeding, sex during menstruation, polygamy, adultery, use of violence, sex with animals, homosexual anal intercourse between men, and many more. The subjects of these lists were always married men, since almost all men of marriageable age were married at that time. Any form of transgression from these instructions was punishable by death.

So these lists and laws were not about condemning same-sex partnerships, since at that time, they were culturally and socially inconceivable. Instead, the overall aim was to prevent the more diverse forms of extramarital sexual activities, as well as adultery and violence on the part of married men.

The hygiene regulations and rules for the protection of marriage and cohabitation had existential significance at that time. Violations were severely punished. Adherence to these rules was also meant to achieve distinction from the sexual practices of the surrounding peoples and cultures. It is interesting that out of all the numerous regulations and purity laws, only the two verses condemning sexuality between men are quoted, and used to create regulations for the 21st century. All other regulations from these chapters are simply disregarded due to the time and cultural distance that has passed.

Romans 1:21–27[20]
21 For although they recognized G*d, they did not honor him as G*d or give thanks to him, but fell into vanity in their thoughts, and their imperishable hearts were darkened. 22 They claimed to be wise and became fools 23 and they exchanged the glory of the incorruptible G*d for images representing a corruptible man and flying, four-footed and creeping animals.

24 Therefore G*d delivered them to uncleanness through the lusts of their hearts, so that they dishonored their bodies by their own doing. 25 They exchanged the truth of G*d for the lie, they worshiped the creature and worshipped it instead of the Creator – blessed is he forever. Amen. 26 Therefore, G*d delivered them to dishonorable passions: Their

---

20   Cf. Lings (2013, pp. 521–564).

wives exchanged natural intercourse for the unnatural; 27 likewise, men also abandoned natural intercourse with women and became inflamed with lust for one another; men commit fornication with men and receive their due reward for their aberration.

The cause of Paul's anger in this passage was not homosexuality. It was just one of a list of stated consequences of unbelief. Instead, Paul was angry with all those who did not worship G*d and were not faithful. The guilt of the people was that they worshipped and praised themselves and their idols; the consequence of this was that people made each other's lives hellish. Paul gave many examples in his catalog of vices. Just one consequence of many was that heterosexual men and women gave up heterosexual sex for sex with someone of the same sex (sexual aberration as a result of unbelief). Paul viewed homosexual acts as one vice among many. This sin was not singled out. Paul addressed his catalog of vices (as a result of unbelief) to all men and women, especially in the port cities of Rome and Corinth. He focused on all the known acts of promiscuity and prostitution at that time.

Paul was concerned with the message of living together respectfully, as Jesus had preached and exemplified in the double commandment of love. Instead of condemning a particular form of sexuality, it is this message that should be enforced.

Pauline catalog of vices sought to address which behaviors should separate G*d's people from other cultures and religions. According to Paul, thieves, miserly persons, blasphemers, drunkards, robbers, murderers and "malakoi oude arsenokoitais" were to be excluded from the kingdom of G*d.

"Malakoi" is the Greek word for gentle, weak, feminine, passive (→ not real men, but "rent boys" and "sissies"). "Arsenokoitais" is the Greek word for male prostitutes and slaves who break laws (they broke the commandment of masculinity not to be passively penetrated by men). The laws were intended to ensure that masculine ideals and patriarchal power structures of the time were not compromised. Common sexual contacts between heterosexual men in the context of (cult) prostitution and slavery (between masters and slaves) were criticized at that time. In the multicultural Roman-Greek culture of the first century, it was not uncommon for male and female slaves to be raped by their male masters and forced into the humiliating role of sex slaves. Paul thus condemned both the practice of male prostitution and pedophilia as well as the practice of sex slaves overall. These practices were subsequently banned by both the early Christian church and Judaism.

1 Corinthians 6:9-10
9 Or do you not know that the unrighteous will not inherit the kingdom of G*d? Do not deceive yourselves! Neither fornicators, nor idolaters, nor adulterers, nor lustful boys (malakoi), nor boy abusers (arsenokoitai) 10 nor thieves, nor the greedy, nor drunkards, nor blasphemers, nor robbers will inherit the kingdom of G*d.

1 Timothy 1:8-11
8 But we know that the law is good if a man uses it rightly, 9 knowing that no law is given to the righteous, but to the unrighteous and disobedient, to the wicked and sinners, to the unholy and reprobate, to the murderers of fathers and murderers of mothers, the manslayers, 10 the fornicators, the boy abusers (arsenokoitai), the traffickers in human beings, the liars, the perjurers,and if anything else stands in the way of sound doctrine, 11 according to the gospel of the glory of the blessed G*d, which is entrusted to me.

These two biblical passages in 1 Corinthians and 1 Timothy also serve as catalogs of vices, in which Paul lists the consequences of straying from G*d and Paul considered male sexual contacts with underage boys one of them. These lists of sins also included adulterers, idolaters, thieves, drunkards, blasphemers, gluttons, and many more. Homosexuality is neither mentioned nor given special attention in these two texts. The catalogs of vices are whole series of transgressions, which Paul said separated people from G*d, without dealing with the individual acts in more detail.

Paul himself had been to port cities such as Corinth several times and would certainly be familiar with the sexual exploitation of minors and slaves and all forms of prostitution. Such sinful behavior was in direct contrast to his way of life at that time. He urged the members of the Christian communities to refrain from the listed vices and to concentrate on worshipping G*d and living together in peace instead. Paul was not concerned with singling out a particular vice, though. Otherwise, he would not have summarized the transgressions in list form.

3 Conclusion

It can be argued that modern ideas of gay, lesbian, bisexual and queer sexualities and relationships were as unknown in the Pauline and post-Pauline periods (circa 50 to 150 A. D.) as they were at the time of the priestly laws in the Book of Leviticus (circa 400–500 B. C.). Therefore, they are not explicitly mentioned in biblical texts. Consequently, the texts of that time cannot and must not be used as a guideline for individual (sexual) behavior, same-sex romantic relationships, partnerships and consensual cohabitation in the 21st century.

For queer-affirming pastoral care, it is important to state this message clearly. For many, however, it is not enough to simply state this. In these cases, it is necessary to go through the individual biblical passages, explain them and place them in the respective context, as I have tried to do in this chapter.

IMPLEMENTATION

VI Queer-affirming pastoral care in the context of ceremonial services

Ceremonial services are church services for specific occasions, such as confirmation, baptism, marriage or funeral ceremonies. They accompany people on important occasions and turning points in their life by means of Christian services and rituals. With regard to queer people, there are other ceremonial services available in addition to the more general ones, such as blessing services or weddings for same-sex couples or naming ceremonies for trans* persons after their transition (see glossary; see also EKHN 2018). Furthermore, based on the topics and given the needs presented so far, traditional services also demand a queer-affirming basis when it comes to queer people or rainbow families. In the following, I will discuss and reflect on some challenges and opportunities.

1 Wedding and blessing services

When services of blessing and wedding ceremonies for queer couples are celebrated in churches, it is not uncommon to share deep conversations and life stories during the preliminary meetings, planning, andduring the celebration itself. These occasions often follow a sequence of pastorally led steps for discussion. Are all family members positive about queer people and their relationships? Are there any conflicts due to that? What experiences have they had with their coming out? Were people hurt emotionally? All these questions play a role in the preliminary discussion for the preparation of a blessing or wedding service, as well as in the selection of the wedding liturgy, the music, and discussions around the service.[21]

When holding preliminary conversations with queer couples, a queer-affirming attitude is just as significant as in any other counseling conversation. In the

---

21 For theological and liturgical reflections on worship services and devotions in the context of same-sex couples and queer issues, see Meister (2019) and Harasta (2016).

following, I will describe the decision-making process leading up to a blessing service in the church congregation I worked in as a parish pastor in Frankfurt. The blessing service took place in 2002, that is, before the Synod (church parliament) of the Evangelical Church in Hessen and Nassau (EKHN) decided in 2003 to officially allow same-sex blessing services. In the years prior to that decision, it was customary for the Church Council of the relevant congregation to decide on a case-to-case basis whether such a blessing service could take place in the congregation or not.

1.1 Request
Two lesbian women, whom I had already met at congregational events, wanted to be blessed by me during a public service in the church. Time was of the essence, as one of them was suffering from terminal cancer. I visited them both regularly and promised them I would raise the issue with the Church Council. My colleague was privy to it, and he supported my request.

Debates in the Church Council
We started an open debate on the topic at the next meeting of the Church Council. After opening the meeting with an introductory theological reflection on the topic, the main debate began. Some members of the Church Council opposed my position, arguing it was impossible to bless a homosexual relationship in church, when the Bible stated that homosexuality was an abomination. We discussed the issue for two hours in an emotionally charged session. Finally, we postponed the decision, which would be made instead at a special thematic session scheduled for the following week. All sides were asked to do some soul-searching in the meantime, to weigh up the arguments once again, and to consider whether the request of the lesbian couple might not be an opportunity to put principles aside and decide in favor of the individuals concerned. In the week that followed, the topic was discussed in all kinds of groups in the district, both inside and outside of the congregation.

The decision of the Church Council
At the special meeting of the Church Council, a number of arguments and concerns were raised once again and explored in greater depth. The debate was less emotional than the week before. Everyone was respectful of those with different opinions. After all the arguments for and against had been presented, we proceeded to vote. A clear majority decided in favor of the blessing for the lesbian couple and also spoke more generally in favor of blessings for gay and lesbian couples in the congregation. A minority of four people were opposed. They rejected these kinds of blessings on theological grounds and they wanted their position documented in the minutes. Everyone accepted this, and

so we ended the special session without creating division among the congregation. We called our agreement "Reconciled diversity."

Preliminary discussions
In the three preliminary conversations with the two women, they told me how they had met and fallen in love, what connected them and why they wanted to be blessed in church.

"Well," K. said, *"I'm not a classic churchgoer or anything. But I grew up religious. My faith is not traditional, but it's there. And because Y. is so sick, it's really important to me that we get blessed as a couple. It's like a sign of protection that we desperately need."*

And when I asked, Y. added: *"I'm more of a free spirit and not church-bound. But since you've been here in the community, something has changed. It has become more open and the topics addressed relate to our lives. I think that's good. And since I know that I don't have much longer to live, it is a matter of my heart to be blessed with K. It is like a seal for our relationship. We would also like to invite all of our friends once more. We want it to be a celebration with G*d's blessing!"*

In the last preliminary discussion, we talked about the Bible text that the two women had chosen. It came from the story of Ruth and Naomi. I had suggested the text to them after having told the story from a queer perspective. A lively conversation followed.

1.2 Queer re-reading of the Book of Ruth[22]

The Book of Ruth is one of the books of the Old Testament.

The beginning of the story
Farmer Elimelech and his wife Naomi of Bethlehem, together with their two sons Machlon and Kiljon, set out to the neighboring country of Moab, because in their homeland Bethlehem was blighted by famine. The road to Moab was long, difficult and full of dangers. But despite the odds they arrived safely and established a new existence there. After some time, one son, Machlon, married Ruth, a Moabite. The other son Kiljon married the Moabite Orpah. Ruth and Orpah were warmly welcomed into the family. Not long after the move to Moab, Elimelech died of a serious illness, followed shortly by Machlon, the first son, succumbing to fever, and the other son, Kiljon, dying in an accident. The three wives Naomi and her daughters-in-law Ruth and Orpah were left alone, leaving their existence in peril, for without men at their side, women were neither legally nor economically protected. As if enough misfortune had not already happened, famine broke out in Moab as well. Naomi decided to return to her native Israel.

---

22 I first published this queer re-reading in: Söderblom (2020a, pp. 46–50).

Departure

Naomi prepared everything and one day she set out on the long journey to her homeland. Her daughters-in-law accompanied her to the border between Moab and Israel which should become a decisive crossroads of life for all three of them. Naomi asked her two daughters-in-law to return to Moab and look for other men to secure their existence. Orpah, after a moment's consideration, turned around in tears and returned to Moab, but Ruth decided otherwise. She promised Naomi to stay with her and serve her faithfully. Ruth thus chose to live with Naomi, even though she knew that two widows alone without men could not survive in those days.

Ruth's Pledge of Allegiance
What Ruth said to Naomi:

"Don't persuade me to leave you. I want to go with you. Where you go, I will go, and where you live, I will live. Your people will be my people, and your G*d will be my G*d. Where you die I will die also, and there I will be buried. G*d may do this to me and that, but only death will separate me from you" (Ruth 1:16).

An interim view

Ruth's statement to her mother-in-law Naomi is remarkable. It is a strong sign of love, loyalty and care. It sounds like a lover's oath of fidelity. In fact, this biblical text from the Book of Ruth has become one of the most popular (heterosexual) wedding oaths over time to this day. It is often used in church weddings. Mostly, however, it is quoted without the participants knowing the context. Very few know that the text is actually an oath of allegiance from one woman to another.

Biblical scholars and exegetes have also pointed out that the word go with (Hebrew "davka") is the same word used in Genesis 2:24 to describe the relationship between a man and a woman in marriage (to cleave to his wife). This fact underscores that the passage is in fact an oath of fidelity (see Lings 2013, pp. 576–579).

In order to understand the sentence, it is important to clarify the context of this statement. The two women lived in a strict patriarchal system where men were in charge and widows without children were considered fair game without protection and economic security. But instead of going back to Moab to find a new husband, Ruth decided to stay with her mother-in-law Naomi. She was willing to learn Naomi's language, accept her G*d and religion, and live in her homeland. She chose to live with Naomi, accepting all the consequences. All who know or have experienced migration stories know how difficult and painful it is.

Queer reading
In a queer reading of the text, Ruth's decision can be seen as a desire for a life covenant, without need for further labels. This form of cohabitation transcended generational, gender, religious, and national boundaries. Some researchers therefore describe Ruth's and Naomi's connection as a love connection. Whether it was so, we do not know. It is in any case conceivable. But it is not even necessary to give this connection a name, because it stands in and of itself. What is clear, is that the two women had forged a particularly close fellowship and cared deeply for one another.

How the story continued
After a long journey the two women arrived safely in Bethlehem. They moved into the empty house of Naomi's deceased husband, Elimelech. Their situation was precarious, as they had no income and no security.

Naomi, though, based on her knowledge of Jewish law and traditional circumstances, had designed a survival strategy. She planned a so-called "levirate marriage" between Ruth and Boaz (see on the Levirate marriage: Deuteronomy 25:5 ff.). Boaz was a brother-in-law to Naomi. In Jewish law, a childless widow was to be married to a brother of the deceased so that the woman could have offspring and be provided for. There was no other way for women to survive at that time. Naomi knew about the right of widows within a levirate marriage and planned it for Ruth. Naomi thus became an actor and director in the subsequent story. Ruth, for her part, trusted Naomi's plan and went along with it. Both were realistic enough to know that they had no other choice if they wanted to survive.

Following Naomi's advice, Ruth regularly visited the wheat fields of Boaz to pick up ears of corn. According to Jewish law, the tenth part of the harvest was set aside for the poor, strangers and widows in order to provide them with a livelihood. After a few days, Boaz became aware of Ruth, inquired about her and became acquainted with her. From then on, he placed her under his protection.

The "redemption"
Again it was Naomi who planned the next step. She instructed Ruth to return to Boaz's tent in the evening and lie down next to him on the bed. Boaz was to "ransom" her by impregnating her. The calculated goal was the marriage of the two.

This is how this familial arrangement between Ruth and the much older Boaz came about. It was an arrangement within the framework of the Jewish law in force at that time. The levirate marriage was something like a social insurance for childless widows.

Boaz thus "redeemed" Ruth so that she could have offspring and, in patriarchal logic, regain a secure position in the community of a family. Thus Naomi was also able to find a place within an economically and socially secure family kinship. The arrangement was also recognized by the other women in Bethlehem. They commented on the development. They praised G*d and thanked Him that Naomi and Ruth had found a "redeemer". Then they cried, *"A son has been born to Naomi"* (Ruth 4:17).

That is a remarkable choice of words. The women did not say that Ruth had born a son to Boaz, but to Naomi. This comment confirms the impression that there must have been a strong connection between Ruth and Naomi and that Boaz was part of this arrangement. But the emotional bond was primarily between Ruth and Naomi.

Ruth and Boaz named their son Obed. He is the grandfather of David, later King David, and the ancestor of Jesus. King David therefore came from a multi-generational blended family.

Concluding remarks

Ruth's love for Naomi dominates this biblical story. Ruth gave up her future in Moab to follow her mother-in-law, Naomi, as a widowed woman. She took it upon herself to live in a foreign country without a secure existence. Love, loyalty and care for Naomi counted more for Ruth than her own fate. The decision was about women's solidarity and mutual care.

Ruth and Naomi are the subjects of this story. They took the initiative. Naomi planned the next steps and Ruth implemented them. They made use of patriarchal jurisdiction, at the same time undermining it by manipulating it to suit their agenda. In so doing, they secured a place for themselves within the system. It was a survival strategy that G*d blessed in the Book of Ruth: Ruth found shelter under G*d's wings (Ruth 2:12), just as she was redeemed under Boaz's robe (Ruth 3:9). The same Hebrew word "kanap" underlines the double protection awarded to her. And by becoming pregnant and having a son, she secured provision for herself and Naomi in their old age, as well as setting in motion a generation leading ultimately to the birth of King David.

The two women became part of a family arrangement, living together with Boaz and their son Obed. Today, one might just call that a rainbow family.

1.3 Resonances

The couple in my case liked the fact that the main protagonists of the book were two women who swore love and loyalty to each other, no matter what else life might throw at them. They also found it impressive that the two later lived together with Boaz and their son Obed in a colorful blended family and in so doing, were able to maintain an unconventional existence in an otherwise patriarchal environment. But what they liked most was Ruth's oath of allegiance.

"That's clearly a declaration of love!" Y. said excitedly. *"I could say the same thing today!"*

"How cool that something like that is in the Bible!" added K.

It quickly became clear that verse 16 from the first chapter of the Book of Ruth would be their biblical verse at the blessing. They both rejoiced and took the verse as a basis to formulate their own promise of faithfulness for the service.

Blessing Ceremony

At the beginning of December 2002, we celebrated the blessing service for the two lesbian women from the congregation. The church was packed. Many of the women and men in attendance came clad in leather, as the couple belonged to a women's motorcycle club in Frankfurt. There were also younger and older women, as well as old and very old men, whom we had never seen before in the church. Some came covered in tattoos and wearing black clothes. Others wore wide batik skirts and colorful scarves. There were men with long hair, women with buzz-cuts, some of them in wheelchairs. They were acquaintances of the terminally ill lesbian, who in the meantime was being treated at the palliative ward of a hospice. Frail and healthy people, nurses and caregivers, and even a doctor from the ward had come to the church. I was proud that the doors of our church were open to such a colorful gathering. This is how it should be. Some church leaders from our congregation were also there. They later said that they had never experienced such an emotional and touching service. The two women gave their wedding vows to each other; there were two maids of honor who wished them well with poems, and I blessed the two women with a rainbow scarf that I placed around their shoulders. There were more than a few tears shed at the church that day. After the ceremony, someone put on a Melissa Etheridge CD and we sang and danced in the church hall. The evening was crowned by a banquet in the hall next door and dance music.

Farewell

Three months later, on Maundy Thursday 2003, after the evening service and communion in the parish, I received a call on my cell phone. One of the nurses who had been present at the blessing ceremony told me that Y. was dying. I apologized to the community members and immediately rode my bicycle to her apartment. About ten people were gathered there. Y's partner K., close friends, a nurse, a neighbor and a brother were present. My partner at the time also joined us. We gathered at the bedside, drank tea and talked quietly to each other. When she opened her eyes once again and was fully present, I held her hands and blessed her with anointing oil I had brought from the Maundy Thursday service. Together we remembered the wonderful celebration of blessing at the church. We wished her well, cried and laughed, and prayed the Lord's Prayer together. Y. listened carefully and felt that she was not alone. All her loved ones were there and everything important had been said. She was no longer afraid of dying. *"It is the way it is,"* she said matter-of-factly.

She smiled as she closed her eyes. Her breathing became quieter and quieter. Shortly before midnight on Good Friday night, she passed away. We formed a circle of blessing, wept, sat with her, and held the wake. The next morning at 10 a.m., I had to conduct the Good Friday service. I knew instinctively that the service would need to take a different format to the one I had planned. That very night I changed some passages in the sermon, added my experience from my night at her deathbed, and wrote an intercession prayer for the deceased and her loved ones. The next morning, I went to the service with bags under my eyes, having hardly slept at all. During the service, K., relatives and friends of the deceased sat in the gallery of the church and wept. They were part of it and thanked me afterwards for having included the experiences of the night before in the service.

"If church was always this close to people, we would rejoin the church", said some of them who had long turned their backs on the church.

At the Easter communion that followed, commemorating death formed an integral part of the service. Again, all the mourners were present and we celebrated the resurrection feast. We were alive in the face of death – despite all of the grief and loss, despite all of the despair and pain. The dead were not forgotten. On the contrary, they were present in our thoughts and prayers while we celebrated the resurrection and the life.

1.4 Conclusion

This case, described in more detail, demonstrates how every aspect of life is present, when people come to us with their life issues and trust pastors and church buildings to be safe and hospitable spaces. While it started out with planning and implementing a blessing service, a wide variety of issues emerged in the process – starting with the theological debate at the Church Council. Following the positive decision of the Church Council, stories from their own lives were explored in the preliminary discussions with the lesbian couple: the process of getting to know each other, relationship issues, coming out in family circles, illness, fears, shared desires and ideas for the blessing service. They were able to relate all of these topics in some way to the troubled story of Ruth and Naomi. They explored the story at length from their perspective and shared it with me. And finally, they decided to take their bible verse for the blessing from the Book of Ruth.

Three months later, Y., one of the two partners, died. Because of the time we had spent together, K. called me to her deathbed. I anointed and blessed the terminally ill, stayed at the deathbed with the others until Y. died. I prayed with the mourners and stayed for the wake. The next morning, I invited the mourners to the Good Friday service. Everyone came. Good Friday thus took on a very concrete quality for the congregation, which touched the hearts of those present and left no one cold. The two lesbian women had become part of the community in the months before. The hospitable attitude of the people in the congregation had made it possible for the two to celebrate their blessing service in the church. A relationship of trust developed, so that I was asked to go to the deathbed to be there with Y.'s relatives and friends and to accompany them in their grief. I also took Y.'s funeral service. After the funeral, I regularly sat alongside Y.'s partner in her grief for another six months. The request for a blessing service for a lesbian couple led to a multi-layered and long-term process of queer-affirming pastoral care, which could not have been predicted at the start. This case shows that queer-affirming pastoral care can play an important role in ceremonial services.

2 Rainbow family baptism

2.1 Request

Two women I had married in a service asked me a few years later if I could bless their son in a service. "A baptism?", I asked back. No, it was about a blessing, they said. They did not want their son to be baptized into the Christian community without being asked. They felt themselves much too distant from the church for that, so their son should be able to decide for himself later. But they would still like to ask for G*d's blessing on him. After all, their faith was important to them, though something quite distinct from the institution of the church. For a while we discussed the church's understanding of baptism and whether the ceremony could be a baptism after all. But they remained firm. They wanted a blessing, not a baptism. They described themselves as critical believers who had distanced themselves from the church due to homophobic abuse, but had not yet lost their faith. They also paid church tax. Was it so presumptuous to ask for G*d's blessing? I understood their arguments and made that clear. It was positive for them, to see their experiences and wishes taken seriously in this way. They finally had a space to discuss their bad experiences. That was important to them. We discussed what a blessing celebration could look like, and finally I agreed to do this. In our next meeting, we planned the blessing service. We also talked about several Bible verses during the process, which ended in them deciding on a suitable one for their son.

2.2 Queer re-reading of Isaiah 43:1b

"Do not be afraid. For I have redeemed you. I have called you by your name, you are mine!"

With this sentence, the prophet Isaiah comforted the people of Israel, who had been in Babylonian exile for more than thirty years at that time (about 550 B.C.). They longed for their homeland Israel but their hope of ever returning was fading. The prophet Isaiah, also called Second Isaiah or Deutero-Isaiah by scholars, because he lived one generation after Isaiah, gave the people in exile confidence and hope with his words. It was not too late, even though they were now living as third-generation exiles far from home in another country, surrounded by a different culture and different gods.

But then political circumstances changed. The Persian King Cyrus II took Babylon and drove out the Babylonian ruler and his soldiers. And it was in this situation that Deutero-Isaiah encouraged the Israelites to no longer despair. They should be confident that they would no longer be subject to the ruler of Babylon nor to the Persian king. His promise became words of protest against oppression and slavery for a whole generation. Deutero-Isaiah underlined his message by presenting the G*d of Israel as the one who had already led Israel out of oppression and slavery once before – namely out of Egypt – at the time of Moses, Miriam and Aaron. G*d was a G*d of freedom! He was a G*d who led people out of oppression and hopelessness and accompanied them through deserts. The promise of the prophet increased their self-confidence and affirmed their desire to return to Jerusalem. In fact, King Cyrus II allowed them to return home shortly thereafter.

To this day, this verse of Deutero-Isaiah is a popular verse for baptisms, as it demonstrates that G*d knows the names of all people. Furthermore, this verse remains a message to all who feel oppressed and alone, either psychologically or politically. In this respect, this verse also serves as an encouragement to every queer person not to be afraid. For G*d is – and remains – a G*d of liberation from oppression and exclusion. This promise applies to everyone, regardless of nationality, religion, gender identity or sexual orientation.

2.3 Resonances

The Bible verse appealed to the mothers. We talked about the strong encouragement that lies in the prophetic statement, about its relevance today, and both of them agreed that it could also be encouraging for queer people, who had experienced exclusion or malice. In this respect, they thought that the verse would be fitting for their son.

The service

We celebrated the blessing at a separate service on a Saturday afternoon at the church where they lived and where we had already celebrated the couple's wedding. The two did not want the blessing to take place at a normal Sunday service, as they feared that church members might take offense. They did not want to be on the receiving end of curious stares, due to the rainbow families who would be present, nor did they want a discussion about the blessing. They had already had more than their fair share of discussions about lifestyles and sexual orientation in church circles and had no desire for more. They still felt uncomfortable and patronized, when they recalled these conversations. So that was decided. On the day of the service, the church was full of rainbow and blended families. Strollers, toys and walkers lined the entrance and the church. Queer friends and relatives were there, creating a colorful melting pot of generations. Children darted in and out of the rows of pews. Two godparents participated in the intercessions, and a musical family of aunts, uncles, nephews and nieces formed their own little orchestra and accompanied the service with music. The grandparents had decorated the church with flowers and the mothers had made a candle for their son. Rainbow and sunlight were the motifs. The liturgical setting was similar to a baptism, except that the son was not sprinkled with baptismal water and not baptized, but blessed. It was a joyful service with a lot of music, a talk by myself which focused on the motives of the two mothers to have their child blessed, which was also tailored to the life story of the family. During the blessing of the son, all the children came forward. They received small candles from me and watched curiously as the son was blessed. At the end, we formed a big circle of blessing in the church. I blessed those present, while the participants each blessed their neighbors to the right with their right hand. The celebration that followed was vibrant and colorful. Everyone present was grateful and happy, that it was possible to hold such a service in the church.

2.4 Conclusion

The mothers' special wish that their son should be blessed in church led to an intensive discussion about their experiences in church contexts. It became clear that both had already been on the receiving end of homophobic remarks and were not sure whether they wanted to be members of the church anymore. Their wedding ceremony and their faith were the reasons why they approached me with their request, nevertheless. However, it was also clear that they would not have just gone to any church community. It was important to them to find a queer-friendly and respectful environment.

The open conversation and my ability to understand their concerns made it possible for a church service to become a colorful and queer-friendly event where everyone felt comfortable. This was an experience that everyone present took home with them. They expressed a desire for all services and celebrations in churches to be like this.

The conversations leading up to the event gave the two women space to discuss the painful discrimination they had experienced in church settings, and enabled them to open up. The exchange about the Bible verse from Deutero-Isaiah strengthened and helped them to feel the promise of G*d for their son and the whole rainbow family. In this respect, the planning discussions contained a pastoral component, which also had an impact on the design of the service and gave all participants the feeling of being welcome, just as they were.

3 Coming out in the confirmation group

As a parish pastor, I have always taught a unit on love and charity in biblical texts and in everyday life in my confirmation classes. In my experience, young people are particularly alert and curious during these units. They naturally want to know how love, and being in love, works and what the others in the peer group think about it and have already experienced. For this reason, I include frequent opportunities for small group work in this unit, offering them a safe space to swap ideas more easily and intimately. But they are also eager to know what the Bible says about these issues and what that might mean today. Since most of the adolescents in my congregation at that time knew from informal sources in the community that I lived with a woman, the topic of "homosexuality and same-sex love" was brought up time and again. They wanted to hear about my experiences and were curious about how I was faring as a lesbian pastor in the congregation. I experienced these conversations as both intense and characterized by genuine interest. Not once did the young people behave in a derogatory or negative way with regard to the subject. On the contrary, they had many questions. After all, how often are you given the chance to ask a lesbian pastor about this? On the other hand, during my time in the congregation, young people repeatedly came up to me after confirmation classes to talk to me personally about these issues. Some of them came out to me as gay or lesbian, others were unsure and simply had questions they would not otherwise dare to ask. The timing of confirmation classes coincides with a key developmental phase for young people, which is crucial for their personal development and for their coming of age. For this reason, a queer-friendly atmosphere in the classroom and a positive approach to different sexual orientations and gender identities is a great source of encouragement for young people. It can encourage them to seek their own way without fear of being wrong or inferior or bad. In the following case study I will tell the story of O. and his coming out to the confirmation group.

3.1 Request

During my time as a parish priest, we talked about the topic of "love and charity" in our confirmation groups. With the help of postcards, youths approaching their confirmation could choose symbols that represented love to them. A heart, a light, a hug, a gift, a love letter, roses, graffiti with the words "I love you!", two intertwined rings and similar motifs. Among them was also a card that showed two boys hugging. A boy, O., picked it. When it was his turn to put his card in the middle of the seating circle and say a few sentences about it, he blushed. The others started whispering, but they were also curious. Finally O. said that two boys or two girls could fall in love with each other. Two girls started giggling, several boys were roaring with laughter. I jumped to O.'s side and confirmed his statement. Of course, two boys or girls could fall in love with each other as well. It doesn't happen that often, but it is quite normal. O. made it clear that he wanted to hear more about it. And the group also wanted to know more. So we agreed to read and discuss a biblical text about it. I suggested the biblical story of David and Jonathan. During our next meeting, we read the story together.

3.2 Queer re-reading of the story of David and Jonathan[23]

The story is set about 1000 B.C. The soldiers of King Saul, the first king of Israel, fought the Philistines, a people that lived on the Mediterranean coast approximately where the Gaza Strip is today. The warring parties fought one battle after another, neither being able to win the upper hand in the conflict. This is the background to the story of David and Jonathan (1 Samuel 28–2 Samuel 1).

David and Goliath

According to biblical testimony, there was a great battle between Israel and the Philistines. Goliath was a huge man and the strongest warrior of the Philistines. He challenged the soldiers of Saul, king of Israel. One of them was to fight him and the winner of that fight would also win the whole battle. When no soldier of the king dared to fight Goliath, David, a young shepherd from Bethlehem, volunteered. He had older brothers who were also involved in the war against the Philistines and he had initially come to provide them with rations. But when he heard the battle announcement of Goliath, he enlisted. He was not wearing armor, nor did he have any weapons. Everyone was horrified and wanted to stop David from fighting Goliath. But he remained undeterred. So the battle ensued. David had a slingshot with him and with one well-aimed shot he hit Goliath in the head. Goliath fell to the ground. David borrowed a sword from a soldier and cut off his head. The battle was over. Saul's soldiers were victorious. Everyone was amazed

---

23 First published in: Söderblom (2020a, pp. 28–34).

by David's courage and fighting spirit. King Saul wanted to know who this David was. He was brought to him. And Saul kept David in the king's court.

Jonathan's Covenant with David
So the young shepherd boy joined the king's court in Jerusalem and there he met Jonathan, one of the sons of King Saul. Jonathan was enthralled by the charismatic David. The Bible says that he loved David like his own life. And as a sign of his love and loyalty, he gave David his armor, sword, bow and belt:

"After David's conversation with Saul, Jonathan took David into his heart, and Jonathan loved David as his own life. He made a covenant with David, for he loved him as his own heart. He took off the coat he had on and gave it to David, as well as his armor, his sword, his bow and his girdle" (1 Samuel 18:1–4).

This biblical passage is remarkable. Jonathan surrendered himself completely to David. He took a high risk. He made himself vulnerable, revealed himself without visor and protection. This was a very untypical behavior for men at that time. What guarantee did Jonathan have that David would not take advantage of this? None. His love knew no bounds. He trusted David. And he even made a covenant with him. David allowed himself to be part of the covenant, even though the biblical passage remains unclear as to what David thought about it.

It was a fateful moment. The king's son swore allegiance to the shepherd's son. What a reversal of hierarchy! Didn't Jonathan realize that he was massively reducing his chances of succeeding to the throne? Didn't he care that as a king's son he was supposed to strengthen his influence and power instead of pledging his loyalty to a man from a simple shepherd's family? What good could come of this?

Issues of status, power and influence stood between them, but Jonathan did not care. He trained David to be a warrior and taught him everything about warfare. And David became a successful warrior. He won battle after battle against the Philistines and became known far beyond the king's court.

Saul's jealousy
King Saul watched this development suspiciously. He did not like the fact that David and Jonathan became best friends. He was also jealous and envious of David. David seemed to succeed in everything he tackled. He had slain Goliath with his cleverness and also remained victorious in further battles. Saul, on the other hand, became more and more melancholic and immobile. He saw his power as king dwindle. David had done a lot for him, but he had become too powerful and popular, which made Saul perceive him solely as a compet-

itor for power and honor. He had to stop David's influence and so he decided to kill him. David had suspected this would happen and had not returned to King Saul's court after a battle.

What happened to Saul was sadly predictable. He realized that what happened to David mirrored something he had experienced as a young man. He had been chosen, anointed and made king. He had been popular, powerful and strong. And now this shepherd's son from Bethlehem had come along and stolen his thunder. He was furious.

Jonathan stands between Saul and David
For his son Jonathan, this must have been a terrible situation. He witnessed his father's anger and despair. And at the same time, he had fallen for David. He was torn between the two and seemed to have forgotten or deprioritized his own future as a potential successor to Saul. Instead, Jonathan stood up for David. He mediated and took David's side. With success. David returned to the royal court.

Saul's curse on Jonathan
But peace proved to be an illusion and Saul fell into melancholy again. When David played the lute for him to cheer him up, as he had often done at the beginning of his time at court, Saul threw a spear at him. As a result, David fled the king's court for good. He set up a secret meeting with Jonathan. Now David took charge. He asked Jonathan to present his father with an excuse as to why David would not appear at a banquet at court. But Saul saw through the ruse and became even angrier. Full of rage, he shouted at his son Jonathan:

"You son of a dishonorable mother. I know very well that you have taken the son of Jesse for yourself. Shame on you and your mother who bore you! But as long as the son of Jesse lives on earth, neither you nor your kingship will endure" (1 Samuel 20:30 f.).

Jonathan's loyalty
Saul cursed his son and called his friendship with David a disgrace. It is a clear indication that Saul knew that friendship was not the only thing between Jonathan and David. He derisively devalued their friendship. Saul sensed the love between David and Jonathan and considered it dangerous, because it broke all the known norms and rules, which were aimed at maintaining power and order in the royal family. Saul became so enraged that he even threw a spear at his own son. It was clear to Jonathan then that the rift between Saul and David could no longer be patched up. The chasm was unbridgeable. The competition between the two had turned into a fight to the death and the ability for Jonathan to act as mediator had passed. He had to make a decision. Outwardly, he remained with his father. But in his heart, he remained on David's side.

Jonathan and David met secretly and renewed their covenant. Jonathan asked David to spare his descendants and those of Saul. Perhaps Jonathan already suspected that he himself had no future at court. Then they took their leave.

Farewell
"David fell on his face to the ground and bowed down three times, and they kissed each other and wept together, but David most of all. And Jonathan said to David: Go in peace! For that which we have both sworn in the name of G*d, G*d may stand between me and thee, between my seed and thy seed forever. And David arose and went his way, while Jonathan went into the city" (1 Samuel 20:41 ff.).

It was the last time the two were to see each other. It is a touching farewell scene and it is told with astonishing frankness. They both kissed and cried. And David the most. Here, for the first time, David's love for Jonathan becomes visible. The two men had to say goodbye. Their love was not allowed to be and had no future. Two men who wept. In keeping with the image of masculinity at that time, this would not end well. They were men and soldiers. They were supposed to be brave and strong. Crying was not part of the deal, especially not crying for each other. That was true then and is still true today in many places. The fact that they also kissed and loved each other did not make things any easier.

We know for a fact from extra-biblical sources that men also had homoerotic love affairs at that time. In fact, it was actually quite common. But at the same time, they had to be married and have children. Men were supposed to be real guys. Homoerotic sex did not contradict this, as long as they did not act in an "unmanly" manner and break with the commonly accepted image of masculinity. They were only considered feminized or effeminate if they appeared too feminine or too sensitive. Then they could expect sanctions and exclusion from the community, since their very existence upset the prevalent gender order.

Remarkable friendship
The story of David and Jonathan must have been unusual even in biblical times. Otherwise, it would not have made it into the Bible in this open language and clarity. What is remarkable, is that their friendship was not condemned or moralized about in the story. Their love was simply there and shaped the actions of the young men, even though they were very different from each other. The Bible tells us, for instance, that David had several wives. He was quite a womanizer. But we do not read of the type of deep love he had for Jonathan in any other place in the Bible.

Lament read from a queer perspective
After the parting of Jonathan and David came another battle against the Philistines. Neither Saul nor Jonathan survived the battle. When David heard about it, he sang a lament:

"Israel, your pride lies slain on your heights. Alas, the heroes have fallen! Saul and Jonathan, the beloved and dear, in life and in death they are not separated. They were swifter than eagles, were stronger than lions. Daughters of Israel, you must weep for Saul, he has clothed you in precious purple, he has pinned gold ornaments on your robes. Oh, the heroes have fallen in the midst of battle. Jonathan lies slain on the heights. I am sorry for you, my brother Jonathan, for I had great joy and delight in you. You were very dear to me. More wonderful was your love for me than the love of women. Alas, the heroes have fallen, the weapons of battle are lost" (2 Samuel, 1 ff.).

This lament makes clear the strength of David's inner devotion to Jonathan. The homoerotic love that dare not speak its name, is clearly audible to attuned ears, but must be cloaked in reverence and coded in terms of praise of bravery and heroism. The language of love was not possible between men. Nevertheless, the end of David's lament is amazingly clear:

"More wonderful was your love for me than the love of women" (2 Samuel 1:26).

One would think that a declaration of love could not be clearer. Especially not in a biblical book that was written centuries before the birth of Christ. And yet this love was dismissed, relativized and pushed to the sidelines. It was labeled as friendship, at best, brotherly love. For what could not be, was not allowed to be. The heteronormative standards did not allow for anything else. The story is simply recorded as a marginal note in the life of David, the courageous and successful shepherd who rose to become king of Israel, and quickly skipped over. That the most famous king of ancient Israel, of all people, loved a man, could not be. Therefore, it should be swiftly forgotten.

The one overshadowing question that remains, is what kind of relationship the two men shared. My answer: it was a relationship that touched me personally. It was a relationship in which the friends made themselves vulnerable and took risks. It was a relationship that disrupted the logic of maintaining power, of male competition, of acquiring fame and honor and countered it with something different: with love, vulnerability, and intimacy. Attributes that were not generally intended for men.

Male friendship

Was this friendship homoerotic? Was it sexual? Were the two men bisexual? Biblical history does not provide any answers here, and also, that is not the point. The point is, this relationship transcends all (hetero)normative male relationships of that time. It tells the story of a touching male friendship. It defies labels and pigeonholes.

And yet one thing is clear: The two men loved each other. They swore allegiance to each other and did not betray each other either, despite all the power play. They trusted each other, kissed each other and cried together.

When relationships are lived this way, they deserve respect. No matter what they are called. Because love is multifaceted, overwhelming, and it can break boundaries. Human feelings are so much richer and more complex than prohibitions and norms, as long as they are based on mutual agreement and with respect for the dignity of the other person.

David and Jonathan show us something about the richness of human feelings. It is good that people can live out such emotions today, even though it is still not easy, or might even be life-threatening, to do so in many places.

3.3 Resonances

The young people found the story exciting. They scolded Saul, thought David and Jonathan were pretty cool, and were sad that Jonathan did not survive the story. They discussed for quite a while whether this story was about more than a friendship. The group was divided on this.

O. said, *"Of course they loved each other. That's what the text says. At least Jonathan had a crush on David. And at the end David showed that he loved Jonathan, too!"*

O. got backing from some. Others didn't think it was so clear. Finally, they agreed that David and Jonathan were close friends and would have done anything for each other. In small groups, they then shared about boy and girl friendships in their lives and collated terminology to describe such friendships. Help, understanding, trust, adventure, fun, time together and other terms were written on the cards. Afterwards, most of them found that such friendships were quite important for them in their lives.

After class, O. came up to me and asked to speak to me in private.

"If you, as a pastor, are a lesbian and that is accepted in the congregation, then I am allowed to fall in love with another boy without that being a bad thing," O. said to me.

"That's definitely true," I replied. *"How can I support you?"*

He told me that he had fallen in love with a boy at his sports club and that the other boy was also in love with him. But it all felt very chaotic and they didn't know what to do. Was it wrong to give in to their feelings? Both were afraid of problems in the sports club and in their school classes.

I talked to them both a few times afterwards and encouraged them not to be ashamed of their feelings. I reminded them of David and Jonathan. Their friendship was in the Bible and it was okay. We know today for a fact, I told them, that a certain percentage of people will fall in love with people of the same sex. That was perfectly fine. But I also admitted that some people, unfortunately, didn't think it was okay. I encouraged them: *"You are unique and special and wonderfully created by G*d just the way you are!"*

I also told them that I had fallen in love with a woman and was living with her. They already knew that, as it was known in the congregation. That had also encouraged the two of them to come to me. They were not afraid that I would judge them. On the contrary, they hoped for understanding and support.

I saw them repeatedly during that year and talked to them about their experiences and questions. Then, one day, O. asked me if I could talk to his parents. He told me that he wanted to talk to them but was afraid of their reaction.

Coming out to parents

Finally, we made an appointment with the parents. I visited them one early evening. We drank tea and sat somewhat stiffly in the living room. In the beginning we talked about my job as a pastor and how I was doing there until we got to the topic, eventually. It became a quiet and open conversation. I asked the parents to listen to their son first and not immediately judge everything he had to say. They complied. O. told them about his feelings of infatuation and his desire not to be afraid or have a guilty conscience about it. After that, the parents asked him and me a whole lot of questions. Finally, we agreed that they trusted their son and allowed him to have his own experiences without judging him. After all, he was their son anyway and a beloved child of G*d. In addition, he should meet with me regularly to be able to talk to me about his experiences without fear. And that is exactly what we did.

> Years later I met O. again at a Pride Parade in Frankfurt. He was now a lot taller than me. He smiled with his whole face and introduced me to his friends.

"This is the pastor who supported me in my coming out. Without her, I would not be who I am today!" He then hugged me affectionately.

3.4 Conclusion

Some young people in the confirmation group knew that I had a female partner. This encouraged them to talk to me about same-sex love as part of the theme "Love and Charity". They were happy to engage with the topic, even though some were nervous or unsure. However, they were probably curious more than anything. But they also got involved because they assumed they could learn more about the topic from an insider. Through the queer re-reading of the story of David and Jonathan and the conversations about it, the confirmands understood that close same-sex friendships already existed in biblical times and that this was perfectly okay. This was new for many. But for O. it was much more than that. It was a liberation. The conversation encouraged him to approach me after a confirmation class and tell me that he had fallen in love with a boy. The trust they both had in me was helpful. The two of them came to me regularly for a while and we talked about everything that was bothering them. As a result, they became more confident and courageous, got to know themselves and their needs better, and no longer felt like outsiders. One day O. asked me to go with him to his parents to support him in his coming out. He had become more confident, but still needed companionship. I gladly went with him. At the meeting it became clear that it was also helpful for the parents to see that a minister could be lesbian without the world ending. They were able to take their son seriously and support him in his personal development without restricting him. My profession as a pastor became an icebreaker between O. and his parents. With me as an example, they saw that being queer and leading a good life can go together. This was important for the parents, who were worried about the future of their son. But they also understood that family and social support were needed. Even though the parents needed time to cope with all the changes, they supported their son in his coming out from then on and he became a self-aware young man. Queer-affirming pastoral care had strengthened him and encouraged him to follow his own path.

4 Naming ceremony in the context of transitions

During my time as pastor and Director of Studies at the Evangelisches Studienwerk (Protestant Scholarship Foundation) in Villigst, I supported several transgender students during their transitions (see Dgti e. V. 2017; EKHN 2018; Lüdtke 2017; Schreiber 2016; Wolfrum 2019). Transitions are complex processes involving gender affirming care with the goal of an individual reassigning to the perceived correct gender. All of the students I was supporting also underwent therapeutic counseling, which they had to complete in line with the Transsexual Act (TSG)[24] in force at the time in Germany. However, they also wanted to discuss issues related to their faith and their transition. They approached me as pastor and chaplain and we arranged individual appointments. In the following, I will describe one case in more detail.

---

24 See Federal Ministry of Justice (1980). Since June 2022, key points for a self-identification law have been available (cf. Federal Ministry for Family Affairs, Senior Citizens, Women and Youth and Federal Ministry of Justice 2022). The Self-Identification Act is to replace the Transsexual Act of 1980.

4.1 Request

At the time of our first contact, X. was studying humanities in southern Germany. We would see each other regularly for counseling sessions over a period of two years.

X. was already in the process of transitioning from female to male, when we met. Initial discussions with close friends had taken place prior to our first meeting. However, most family members and friends hadn't been informed yet. X. described himself as clumsy and hard like a stone. He was afraid of the reaction of family and friends and wondered what effect the transition would have on his faith.

In our first meeting, X. likened his situation to a jewel set in a stone that was just below the surface. However, it was neither visible nor perceptible to X. On the one hand the jewel had to be protected, on the other hand it wanted to come to the surface and be seen.

Over the course of the counseling, X.'s transition progressed further and he also attended the therapy sessions required by the TSG continuously.

After a while he started HRT (hormone replacement therapy) for his transition and from then on wanted to be addressed as C., pronouns he/him.

C. used the counseling sessions with me to talk about problems and times of crisis during his transition and their impact on his studies. It required guidance on a personal and professional level. He wanted to reflect on the motives and motivation for his transition and learn to feel and express his feelings relating to his hopes and fears about his desire for change. In addition, C. wanted to relate his physical and emotional changes to his faith.

"At the church where I was a team leader as a teenager, someone like me was unthinkable. There was consensus that everyone who was homo or somehow different did not fit into G*d's creation and had already been damned in the Bible. This troubles me. For me it is clear that I am C. My gender reassignment is going to happen. But I don't know how and where my faith fits in."

Taking time

We took a lot of time to explore what C.'s faith had looked like pre-transition and what effect the experience as a young team leader in the congregation had had. Fellowship, excursions and church services had proved the most important experiences for him as a congregant. But if he now came back to the congregation as C., the previous bond would be broken. The people there wouldn't understand and would reject him, of that C. was sure. When asked if he had ever spoken to anyone from the congregation, C. denied it. He would first have to come to terms with G*d and the changes he was making to his life. So we took our time to talk about the changes he had noticed in himself since beginning his transition. In this context, C. still described himself as a hard and misshapen stone. The surface had to be hard. For him, this meant protection from harm.

But the hard surface also took away his ability to feel what else was there. For our next meeting, he brought a hand-sized stone, partly angular, partly rounded, iridescent in various shades of gray.

"That's how I feel – gray, edgy, off-putting!" said C.

I asked him to put other things next to the stone that could change the hardness of the stone without taking away the protection. The next time he brought a feather and a rose blossom on a thorny branch. He put everything next to the stone and tried to relate what he saw and felt.

Values and resources

At the same time, we worked on values that were important to him. C. mentioned community, friendship, and his faith. However, his old peer group was no longer around and at the moment he preferred not to meet new people whom he would only unsettle later. His faith had also somehow begun to waver. I asked him about the resources he had used so far when he was in conflict or crisis. Sports and reading he answered. We agreed that he would be more proactive about walking and going to the gym regularly. Then he put together a reading list for himself: some biographies of trans* people, crime novels to distract him, and a sociological book on queer theory.

He commented that he also wanted to change something within his humanities studies. He felt there was a lack of critical analysis of heteronormativity and the gender binary in the seminars. After his Bachelor's degree, he considered pursuing a Master in Gender Studies. He wanted to become more articulate, not only in terms of understanding himself, but also in terms of societal debates.

During one of our next meetings, we talked about the biblical story of the Ethiopian eunuch. C. had asked me to pick out a biblical story that dealt with such a topic, and was surprised to find that there were passages in the Bible concerning this.

4.2 Queer re-reading of the story of the Ethiopian eunuch[25]

The story of the Ethiopian eunuch appears in Acts 8:26–39. At that time, a eunuch was either a castrated man or a person ambiguous in their gender representation. And the story goes like this:

Jesus was no longer there. Now the disciples and all the other believers around Jesus had to carry his life story and message into the world. They had to be courageous, persevering and they had to relate Jesus' message in their own words. But above all, Jesus had told them to go to the people and baptize them in the name of the Father and of the Son and of the Holy Spirit (Mathew 28). This was their mission. The first non-Jewish

---

25 First published in a longer version in: Söderblom (2020a, pp. 35–38).

convert reported in the Acts of the Apostles was a black tax official from Ethiopia. And as a eunuch, he also belonged to a minority.

According to the biblical story, the apostle Philip was traveling on a desert road when he met an Ethiopian chamberlain that the Bible described as being a eunuch. On his way back from Jerusalem, he was sitting in a chariot reading a chapter from the book of the prophet Isaiah, when he saw Philip. The stranger invited Philip to join him in his chariot and there Philip told him about Jesus and his message. The eunuch listened attentively. His interest was aroused and by the end of the story, he was completely enthralled by the stories about Jesus. He showed Philip a body of water that lay by the side of the road, and said, *"Look over there. There is water. What else stands in the way of my baptism?" (Acts 8:36).*

He wanted to be baptized by Philip, so he did and then went on his way.

Traditionally, the story is used to encourage believers to tell people they encounter about Jesus and his message, so that they could perhaps convert them, lead them on the right path or even save them. The fact that the chamberlain was a eunuch is often omitted in this context, thus his ambiguous gender identity is concealed because it does not fit the picture.

Thus, the queer re-reading of the text is first of all about making this circumstance visible. The chamberlain was not only black and from abroad, but he was also a eunuch.

Meeting at eye level
I am convinced that the story of the Ethiopian eunuch is not solely about a person being baptized and converted by Philip, but rather about the fact that Philip was impressed by the eunuch when they met face to face. When he met Philip, the eunuch was reading from the Book of Isaiah, so he seems to have been someone knowledgeable in the Jewish scriptures. Perhaps he was even a Jew and perhaps he also knew the lines from Deuteronomy, according to which no so-called "emasculated" or "castrated" person could be in communion with G*d (Deuteronomy 23:2). The law forbade eunuchs from entering the temple. Since they did not fit into any of the designated categories, they were considered "unclean." They did not have a place in the Holy of Holies. Nevertheless, the eunuch had traveled to Jerusalem to pray.

On his way back, he met Philip, of all people. And he baptized him. He baptized him because the eunuch had asked him to. Philip did not start arguing that one had to be this or that, or have done this or that before, in order to be baptized. Nor did he say that a eunuch could not be baptized. He simply did it. The encounter with the eunuch must have impressed him. Maybe it made him think, maybe it even touched him personally. Perhaps it was also through the eunuch that Philip found out what it really means to seek G*d, for he had met someone who, against all odds had continued to search for G*d. We do not know. What we do know is that Philip baptized the stranger. A black eunuch from a foreign country, of all people.

4.3 Resonances

The story fascinated C. He was thrilled that the eunuch was baptized by Philip, even though he was a foreigner, black, and a eunuch.

"What a cool story," he said afterward. *"I didn't know that one. A eunuch was baptized and belonged to Christianity without any problems. Wow!"*

"Yes, exactly. Because all people are created in G*d's image, regardless of their origin, skin color, gender identity and sexual orientation!", I added.

C. was beside himself about the fact that this was a story from the Bible.

"So it's not a contradiction at all: being non-binary and being Christian?",
he asked.

"That's just it!", I answered firmly. C. smiled.

"I'm going to remember this story. I feel something has been set in motion inside of me. I no longer feel as clumsy, and angular like the gray stone. Suddenly I'm allowed to shimmer a little. That feels amazing!"

We also talked about the Bible passage and other biblical statements about eunuchs at the next meeting. In the meantime, more than a year passed. The gaps between our meetings grew longer and each time I saw C., he had progressed further in his transition. His voice had dropped, his face was more angular, and he had grown stubble for the first time. At the end of the second year, C. wanted me to celebrate a naming ceremony for him at a church service. We had talked about the possibility beforehand. In the meantime, C. had joined a support group for trans* people and was able to explore his questions, problems and fears with them. He was much more self-confident, but he still referred to himself as a stone, even though it had become much more colorful and beautiful and had also acquired soft spots, with intricate filigrane patterns. That's how C. explained it to me, smiling mischievously.

Naming Ceremony

We agreed to celebrate a naming ceremony within the framework of a service at the University Chaplaincy. We wanted to symbolize and celebrate the solemn transition from his old name to the new. The Bible text was to be the story of the Ethiopian eunuch, and C. himself wanted to explain what the story meant to him. He also wanted to invite some members of his support group along. One of them played the piano and wanted to contribute the music for the service.

"These won't be church songs or anything, but improvised pieces that I wrote myself," the friend said to me in the preliminary conversation. At the center of the service, we planned for me to pronounce C.'s new name and pronouns and bless him. With these elements included, we continued to shape the service. C. invited some friends and even family members whom he had told about his transition. Most of them were surprised, but reacted relatively calmly to the changes. Only his parents were worried that C.'s life would be much more difficult from now on. Many came that day. Two friends had already decorated the church with rainbow flags, candles and flowers on the chairs. His friend improvised on the piano as planned and two people from his trans* group read out loud good wishes and an intercessory prayer for his life with a new name. After the service, we celebrated with champagne and cake in the church annex, and toasted C. I don't think I had ever seen him so happy as he appeared on that afternoon and I was grateful for having been able to accompany him on this part of his journey.

4.4 Conclusion

It was important for C. that we met face to face and that I understood his concerns and fears. He profited from being able to speak freely without fear of making himself vulnerable. The search for symbols was meaningful for him. It allowed him to develop images for his transition. It helped him to think about who he was and how he wanted to express himself.

The decisive turning point in our process was talking about the biblical story of the Ethiopian eunuch. It was a great surprise for him to find out that there was a biblical story he could relate to and this strengthened him. Through the Bible story, we started our conversation about a naming celebration for him. The eunuch in the story was baptized for the first time, but C. had already been baptized. As he had already changed his name, he wanted a celebration to show that he now belonged to the Christian community with a different name.

The planning and execution of the service became the highlight of his transition process up to this point. It meant a lot to him, especially since he was actively involved in it. He told everyone present what the biblical story meant to him and was proud of it.

Queer-affirming pastoral care and walking alongside them can support the personal development of queer people. Re-reading biblical stories from a queer perspective can be a perfect means of encouragement and strength.

5 Queer funeral services

In my various pastoral ministries, I have held a few funeral services for queer people or had bereavement conversations with queer relatives and friends. In these conversations, it is especially important that pastors are sensitive to signs that might indicate that the deceased was, or the bereaved are, queer. Queer-affirming pastoral care is mindful of these signs and consciously addresses them throughout the process of preparing for and conducting funeral services. In these settings it is vital to keep in mind that relatives might not always know that the deceased were queer and that they also might not wish this to be addressed in the spoken reflection. The result is a balancing act, as queer partners and friends of the deceased also need to be mentioned without being concealed or ignored. This is sometimes not easy and might, especially in situations of sudden bereavement and shock, present great challenges to those affected. A queer-affirming attitude and a friendly, and at the same time calm, handling of these topics can help to offset the fears and worries of those involved and create dignity within the process. However, this is not always successful, as I know from my own experience. This leads me to recollect a funeral service that was not easy in the run-up to it, but which had a good outcome in the end

5.1 Request

I was still a parish pastor in Frankfurt when I met L. at a conference on physical and mental health of queer people in Berlin. L. was in my small group. Since he was also from Frankfurt, we quickly got talking. Over the course of the weekend, he told me about himself. L. was gay and HIV positive but due to his medication, he was now living quite well with it. Recently, however, he had been diagnosed with an autoimmune disease that weakened him. He felt that the mixture of HIV and the new disease was taking a toll on him mentally and physically. He worked for a company where his co-workers did not know that he was gay and HIV positive.

"I've just had too many negative reactions and rejections in my life due to outing myself," he explained.

L. had a partner, B., whom his family did not know.

"My parents are so conservative, they would freak out if they heard that," he continued. I nodded.

"I'm from a conservative Protestant home in rural Hesse, where life still follows a completely different pace than in the city!" he laughed.

We kept in touch loosely after the conference, writing e-mails and meeting at a queer bar in Frankfurt from time to time.

Death and mourning
Two years after we met at the conference, his partner B., whom I had also met once, called.

"L. is dead!" he said in a broken voice. *"He died of a heart attack. Can we meet?"*
We set a date to meet at a queer-friendly bar.
"It all happened so fast. I didn't even get to say goodbye properly!"
B. had tears streaming down his face. *"I found him on the floor of his apartment and immediately called 911. But he was already dead by then. What am I supposed to do now?"*
I was shocked and told him so, while offering my condolences. I had no more words. I listened to him faltering, stuttering, crying and telling me more.

At some point he asked, *"Would you take the funeral service? Please. I know that L. would have wanted it that way. And I don't know at all how I should act towards his parents. They don't know anything about me. They think that their son was single and I'm sure they want to control everything with the funeral. I can't explain it all to them."*

I replied that the funeral would indeed be arranged with the next of kin. Since the two men were neither married nor in a civil partnership, it was not possible for B. to arrange it. The authorities would probably contact the parents.

But I promised to get in touch with them.

Talking to the parents
It was a difficult conversation. I had made arrangements over the telephone and then went to their village in Hesse. They were grieving for their son – shocked, stunned and totally stressed out. At the same time, they were busily going about organizing the whole funeral, arranging to have their son buried in the Hessian village.

I took a deep breath and explained to them that there was a close relative in Frankfurt with whom everything had to be clarified.

"What? And who is that supposed to be?" they asked.

I told them about B. and that the two of them had been in a committed relationship for over ten years. I proceeded to explain that their son had not dared to tell them in his lifetime.

The silence that followed was deafening. After what felt like an eternity, the mother began to cry while the father blushed and yelled: *"I forbid you to tell such lies about my son! He is not a homosexual. We would have known. That B. can go to hell. He has nothing to do with our son! Our son will be buried here, so we can tend the grave. End of story!"*

Silence. After a while, I expressed understanding for their shock at the surprising news. I remained calm and asked them to think about what it would mean for the partner if they simply ignored him after ten years of relationship, just to keep up false appearances.

And with that I took my leave. I felt that enough had been said. As I said goodbye, I explained that I would call again in a few days. In fact, the conversations went back and forth by phone over the next few days. Grief ate away at the parents, but also the shock that they had known so little about their son.

Finally, the parents agreed that the son should be buried in Frankfurt and that I should take the funeral service in the chapel at the main cemetery. A funeral director was contacted and an urn was selected.

The parents did not want the neighbors and their community to know about their son's sexual orientation. This was also not to be mentioned in the funeral reflection. Again, I explained in a friendly but clear way that I would have to discuss this not only with them, but also with B. But I promised them that I would handle all the information with utmost discretion.

Before the funeral service, the parents and B. met in my office at my request. I had suggested it and all three had agreed after some time for reflection.

Meeting and planning the funeral service
B. told the parents about their son and how the two had met and fallen in love. He showed them photos of how they had been in a relationship together for the past ten years without sharing an apartment, which they had considered too risky.

B. explained that L. had consciously decided not to tell his parents because he feared their reaction. The parents remained silent and listened. After an hour, I put on a second pot of tea and left the three of them alone. They seemed to get along quite well. After yet another hour, they agreed that B. should be mentioned as a partner in the funeral reflection.

B. wanted music by Leonard Cohen, the singer they both liked very much. The parents were open to it.

"How about the title 'Anthem'?", I asked.
There's this line in it that I like a lot:
"Ring the bell, that still can ring. Forget your perfect offering.
There is a crack in everything. That's how the light gets in."

I explained my thoughts on this. I said: *"Especially in mourning or in times of crisis, people often no longer see the light at the end of the tunnel. The light just doesn't reach them anymore. But, as Leonard Cohen sings, it is precisely through the cracks of what is broken and painful that a little light comes in. It finds its way. That's how I understand Leonard Cohen's lyrics."*

5.2 Queer re-reading of John 8:12

B. and the parents nodded. They agreed that I should interpret the text in my talk. Now only a Bible verse was missing. This was very important to B. I took out a collection of Bible verses that I always had with me for bereavement talks. I pointed to one that took up the light theme of Leonard Cohen.

"How about this Bible verse?", I asked, reading aloud:

"I am the light of the world. Whoever follows me will not walk in darkness, but will have the light of life" (John 8: 12).

The others also read the verse aloud and let the content sink in. After a while, I continued speaking:

"Jesus promised people light through his message. Not the glaring light of a bright, sunny day, not the glare of a spotlight, but the little bit of light that glows through the cracks and keeps the spark of hope alive. Just exactly what Leonard Cohen sang about."

I had already experienced a moment like that myself and thought to myself that it is precisely this little bit of light that means so much to many queer people. Because they often don't dare to step into the bright spotlight, just as they are. Just as L. had not dared to come out to his parents. And precisely for that reason I was convinced that Jesus' encouragement especially applies to those who are so often left in the dark.

5.3 Resonances

B. and the parents agreed with my suggestion regarding the Bible verse.

"There were so many times when I really didn't see the light anymore," B. responded to my words. *"This double life wore me down. L. was very timid. His religious upbringing had a strong influence on him and that made it impossible for him to come out to his family. I accepted that and adapted. But I did not feel good about it. I can hardly believe that I'm sitting here with L.'s parents, planning his funeral service with them. I would never have thought that! After L.'s death, of all things, a small ray of light comes into my life, despite all the sadness. I lost L. and found his parents. What madness!"*

L.'s parents were silent at first. But I could tell from their faces that they were now ready to see their deceased son for who he was, and not just a glorified version of him. What was also clear, though, was that they would need a lot of time to digest all of this. There was still enough room for the parents to talk about their memories of their son. And we discussed what I should mention in the mourning speech.

The funeral service

My conversations with the parents and B., my thoughts on the song lyrics of "Anthem", and the scripture from John 8:12 were woven into a personal address at the funeral service. There were some friends of L. and B. who were grateful that L.'s being gay and the two sharing a life was not covered up. Vice versa the parents, and some distant relatives were relieved that L. received a loving funeral service and that some of the parents' memories of their son also appeared in the reflection.

After the funeral service, most of them went to a nearby café. The parents had invited them. It was a colorful mixture of people from a Hessian village and queer people from the big city. I looked at the colorful picture from the counter for a while and thought, church should always be this colorful.

5.4 Conclusion

Because of the encounter with a gay man and his partner, I was asked whether I would take the funeral service for L. when he died. I met with the grieving partner, took my time and spoke to the parents as well. They had not known until then that their son was gay. The conversations that followed were difficult and painful. But my appreciative attitude toward them and my advocacy for the partner made it possible to enter into a dialogue against the odds and finally even to plan the funeral service together. What followed became a meaningful process for all involved. It left room to acknowledge pain, grief and loss and to show these in front of others. The sharing and planning of the funeral service had strong pastoral care components. The queer-affirming atmosphere during the conversations enabled the parents to subsequently accept their son as he was.

6 Conclusions

All five of these case studies involving religious ceremonies show that pastoral conversations can play an important role, either on the sidelines or at the center of preparation for ceremonial services. In ceremonies connected to queer issues, be it a same-sex blessing or wedding, or queer people involved in baptisms, blessings, confirmations or funerals, a queer-affirming pastoral attitude is just as important as queer-affirming behavior.

In the first example of the blessing of a female couple, the blessing service would probably not have happened at all, had the entire Church Council, my colleague and I not argued to hold the blessing service. A few months later, I had to take the funeral service for one of the two partners, and I walked alongside the grieving partner as a chaplain for quite a while, without avoiding queer issues.

I was able to prepare for, and carry out, the blessing of the son of a female couple, as space was given to criticism of the church as an institution, and because queer issues could be discussed, and were not taboo.

In confirmation classes, too, the topic of same-sex love could be discussed in depth, and a young gay person was able to come out of the closet because the young people generally trusted me to deal with the topic in a queer-affirming way.

C. would probably not have approached me to support him through his transition had I not already made it clear in sermons and in other statements that queer-theological issues were a matter of the heart for me. The same was the case in the funeral service for the gay man whose parents neither knew that their son was gay nor that he had a partner.

The role of chaplain was significant in the pastoral care given in all of the ceremonial services described. In addition, the exploration of biblical texts from a queer perspective was helpful in all of these case studies, as they facilitated the processing of life stories. Most of the people were surprised that there were biblical stories they could relate their life to. The occasion-based support of people at important junctures in their lives ultimately took on a power of its own and touched everyone involved. Celebrating and laughing together, praising and singing, criticizing and questioning, weeping and mourning, lamenting and comforting, crying and being silent are essential parts of life. When they include queer people, and are carried out with a queer-affirming attitude, they can serve as encouraging and empowering experiences. They are the foundations of queer-affirming pastoral care throughout the life cycle.

VII Queer-affirming pastoral preaching

Short devotional readings, sermons and meditations do not only occur in church services but also during visits to the sick, at Christian conferences, during morning devotions on the radio, as short reflections in introductions to workshops or training events, at church conventions, and in many other places. They often have a pastoral component. Or to put it another way bible readings and sermons may lead to pastoral care situations in the form of follow-up discussions, and these can sometimes lead to longer-term pastoral support. When the sermon highlights biblical and everyday topics from a queer perspective, it sends a clear signal to queer people that they are welcome with their questions and issues. It lowers the barrier for queer people to turn to counselors. This is because sermon content delivered from a queer perspective provides a concrete starting point for queer-affirming pastoral care. In the following, I present some sermons from a queer perspective that I have delivered in different contexts and I present some comments and reactions to these.

1 "Get up and walk!" – The healing at the pool of Bethesda told from a queer perspective

1.1 Sermon

The basis of this sermon is a scripture from John 5:1–9. I preached this sermon at an ecumenical lesbian conference at the Protestant Academy in Bad Boll, Germany.[26] Following the sermon, there was ample time for discussion in small groups and a subsequent follow-up discussion in the plenary session.

In a small town

He had been alive for 38 years now, 38 years of leading a double life. How could it have come to this? Kai had not yet managed to come clean and tell it like it really was. Until now, the benefits of saying nothing was greater than the liberation of finally speaking up. But it had made Kai ill. Sick in his soul, sick in terms of his self-esteem. Sick because his double life was sickening. He despised himself deeply because he had betrayed himself and his loved ones. Yet, he did not dare to speak the truth.

He had grown up knowing that being gay was perverted, sinful, disgusting, sick. It was not allowed under any circumstances. And anyone who felt that way was not worthy of being part of society. That's what he had heard in the schoolyard, that's what he had heard in his church youth group, that's what he had heard from his parents. But he wasn't disgusting, perverted or sick at all. He wasn't like that. And if he didn't say it and live it, no one would notice, would they? So from then on he tried everything to hide his true feelings. He wore a mask and became sick in body and soul. And he stayed that way. The benefit of saying nothing and not revealing himself outweighed the relief of finally letting it all out.

By the pond of Bethesda

A sick man was sitting at the Pool of Bethesda for 38 years. It was a place where the sick could be healed. He himself could not get up and could not walk. He was 38 years old, but he looked like sixty. He was dirty and his clothes were rags. His skin was dry and wrinkled, he had countless lines on his face and looked terrible. He smelled abysmally and just wanted to escape. But so far, even with the help of others, he had not managed to be the first in the pool when the water moved, and then submerge himself. But he had

---

26 First published in: Söderblom (2020a, pp. 14–18).

to do that in order to be healed. So it was said. He was always too late. Someone else was always faster. Something else always came up. So he became weaker and weaker. After 38 years, he was still sitting there, disgusted with himself, waiting.

Healing

One day Jesus came to him and asked him:

"Don't you want to get better?"

In response, the man repeated his tale of woe. He wanted to explain. He wanted to say why he was sick and couldn't do anything about it, why he hadn't managed to get to the pool first, why he was still sitting there. He wanted the stranger to understand him. The stranger listened and then said:

"Get up, take your mat and go!"

At first the man did not understand. But Jesus looked at him, unwavering. Then he tried it. His joints cracked, his legs buckled. But he kept going. Amazed, he found that he could actually stand up. All by himself. He was afraid he was about to fall over again. He swayed and looked around uncertainly. He stank, and in his dirty rags he looked terrible. He felt ashamed and was panting terribly. He was not used to standing. But it worked. In spite of everything. It was basically impossible, but here he was, standing. He could actually stand and walk on his own two feet after 38 years. A miracle had happened. He had made it.

In disbelief, he took his mat and told everyone who would listen about his experience. He was unsure what he should actually say. It was all so overwhelming. How had the stranger done it? And how had he done it himself? He didn't know how to live without sitting. He had always been sick and now this. He was afraid of how things would change, because everything was so different now. But he was also happy and grateful that he could move.

Fear

For a while now, Kai had been engaging in meditation at a church congregation not far from his workplace once a week: Breathing exercises, sitting in silence, taking a word of prayer with him into the silence. At the end of each session there was a word of blessing from the pastor. It did him good. He became calmer. He tried to recall his prayers from before. But he did not succeed. Silence remained. Breathe in, breathe out. During a meditation session, in silence, he heard a voice within:

"Kai, do you want to get better?"

"Yes, I do," he said to himself. And he continued to speak to himself:

"But my fear is just too great. What will my wife say? And what will my parents say when they find out I love men? I know their negative views on homosexuality. And how will my employer react when they find out that I am gay? They'll kick me into the gutter.

They'll shun me and make fun of me. They will call me things: 'Haha ..., he's a fag, he loves men, he's a fucking faggot."

Inner struggle
The inner voice persisted:

"Kai, do you want to get better?"

And so his inner dialogue continued:

"Yes, but I don't dare. My wife doesn't know anything. I have only had gay sex in secret. No steady relationships, not even spoken about it. I'm living a double life, and it's making me sick. I have an ulcer. My double life has literally punched me in the stomach. And I have buzzing in my ears, as if my ears don't want to hear my lies anymore. I sleep badly, feel lethargic and have no drive to do anything. I struggle with depression. But I'm not seeing a therapist, and I'm not seeing a doctor. I know where it comes from. If I were to come clean with my wife, my parents, my friends and my colleagues, then ... Yes, then what? I just don't have it in me. I feel sick. But as sick as I am, I still feel better than if I were honest. Then my whole life would be destroyed."

Again his inner voice spoke up:

"Kai, get up and open your mouth now! Go and fix your life. Get up and get well!"

Kai was stunned and disturbed. He had never heard such a clear announcement. After the meditation session, he was all agitated. He asked the pastor to talk. Everything burst out of him. The minister listened to him, nodded understandingly and advised him to tell his wife the truth. She also offered to speak with him again, if necessary.

After the conversation, he put on his jacket and went out into the street. He walked around aimlessly for what felt like hours. Then he made a decision. He had been waiting for this moment for a long time. And then he did it. He told his wife, talked to his best friend on the phone, and then to his parents. Over the next few weeks, he visited everyone who was important to him and told them what needed to be said. He cried and stuttered, breaking off sentences and starting over. And then it was finally out.

Horror
When he told his wife, there was silence at first. She was shocked, horrified and stunned. Then she became angry and shouted at him:

"Why didn't you tell me this before? Why did you put on an act for me? Why did you lead a double life? With other sex partners and the Full Monty? It makes me sick just thinking about it. Why didn't you trust me, or at least a therapist? Don't worry, you being gay isn't the problem. But if you had been honest, you might have lived very differently, with me or without me, I don't know. In any case, you should have admitted the truth to yourself and to the world. You were living a lie and dragged me into it!"

Kai couldn't say anything in reply, there was no explanation. He listened to his wife's tantrum and nodded. He could understand her. She was right. His mind was blank and he had no words. Still, he could also understand why it had taken him so long to open his mouth. Only he couldn't explain it.

Gone was the mat of a double life
So now he had gotten up. He had pulled away his comfortable mat of a double life and the floor under his feet vanished. It was terrible, painful, and he was ashamed. Why had he waited for so long? Why had he been that untruthful?

His wife was angry, hurt and wanted nothing more to do with him. He was inconsolable and sad. But if he was honest, he was also relieved, despite everything. Finally, it was out. He had finally said what he had been afraid to say for years. It had been hard, and he had hurt his wife and parents. But somewhere deep inside, he also knew it was the right move. Yes, he should have done it much sooner. He probably shouldn't have gotten married at all. But he loved his wife. Life wasn't just black or white. It was all much more complicated and tangled. And he had hoped that his lethargy and listlessness would eventually pass. He had waited and waited. And in the process, he had become ill.

Life between shards and hope
And now it was out. His life was a shambles. But deep inside he also knew that he could now look at himself in the mirror again. With wounds and scars, with wrinkles, disheveled hair and stubble. This was his only chance to heal ultimately. Maybe his stomach ulcer would subside, his ears and soul would be at peace. He also knew that he needed professional help for that. He would take care of that.

Whether he would ever be reconciled with his wife, he didn't know. But he had understood something: Only by being honest with himself could he possibly manage to be reconciled with himself and others and live a life of dignity.

1.2 Resonances

Many of the bisexual, lesbian or queer conference participants were no strangers to feelings of fear, anxiety and shame. Quite a few of them were married and had children themselves. Some had always known they were different, but it had not been possible for them to talk about it. The church, social pressure and heteronormative rules had been too strong. But above all, the fear of rejection, malice and other negative reactions was too intense. Which is why the benefits of not saying anything was also sufficiently attractive to some of the participants, even though they longed for a different life.

Others had come out early or not at all. The latter had been afraid to be pigeonholed. What they all shared, though, was the concern that they would experience rejection or even suffer professional repercussions if they came out as lesbian, bisexual or queer. Staying silent and invisible was therefore a bittersweet way to live one's life without making a splash and without having to break with heteronormative rules. Some, however, paid a high price for it, both mentally and physically. Invisibility and double lives cost life energy, create feelings of guilt and shame, and lead to illness and depression.

The issue of whether being ill was worth the benefits of staying quiet, which was addressed in the sermon, moved many participants and sparked intense conversations. They shared their fears and hopes, and some shared their stories of liberation after coming out. In a way, they became each other's temporary queer-affirming therapists. For some, it marked the beginning of life changes. I walked alongside one woman as a counselor for a longer period of time after the conference.

2 "Come out!" – The raising of Lazarus told from a queer perspective

2.1 Sermon

The biblical basis to this sermon can be found in John 11:1–45. I delivered the reflection during a workshop at an ecumenical lesbian conference at the Protestant Academy in Bad Boll.[27] A woman read the biblical verses, while I read out loud my thoughts about the verses. After the reflection, we took a lot of time in small groups to absorb and process the feelings of the listeners, and how the reading and reflection had resonated with them. Afterwards, I had personal one-on-one conversations with two women on the topic.

Sick
1 Now one was lying sick, Lazarus from Bethany, the village of Mary and her sister Martha. 2 Now Mary was the one who had anointed the Lord with anointing oil and dried his feet with her hair. Her brother Lazarus was sick.

Sick. Hiding makes you sick, not speaking up makes you sick. Living a double life. Not being able to be honest. "Yes, my best friend is going on vacation with me." – "How nice that you don't have to go alone." Putting a brave face on a desperate situation. Hidden away, I feel safer. Who knows what else the family, neighbors, boss will say. I don't feel safe. It makes me sick.

---

27 The reflection is inspired by a sermon on the Bible text by Birgit Mattausch and a radio devotion by Sandra Zeitler. First published in: Söderblom (2020a, pp. 19–25).

The one you love
3 Then the sisters sent to Jesus, saying, Lord, behold, he whom thou lovest lieth sick.

The one you love. Jesus loves Lazarus. Lazarus loves Jesus. Meaning: They like each other. They understand each other. More is not possible. Anything else is unthinkable. Is unseemly, immoral, impossible. Jesus, the Son of G*d. Of course, he loved all his loved ones. Didn't he say: Love your neighbor as yourself? There you go. Over interpretation is forbidden. "To love" has two sides. Two very different sides. Jesus loves Lazarus. Lazarus loves Jesus.

It takes time
4 When Jesus heard this, he said: This sickness is not unto death, but for the glorification of G*d, that the Son of G*d might be glorified thereby. 5 Now Jesus loved Martha and her sister and Lazarus. 6 When he heard that he was sick, he stayed two more days in the place where he was.

Delay. There is lead in my shoes. The faster I run, the further away the goal seems. I want to go. But I am slowed down. By another appointment, another obligation. Constraints. Responsibility. I can't get away. Every step a struggle. Every step wobbly, too much. It takes … too long.

Stoning
7 Then he said to the disciples, "Let us go back to Judea. 8 But the disciples said to him, "Rabbi, just a moment ago the Jews wanted to stone you, and you want to go there again?

Stoning. He is different. He is strange. He irritates people. He does not play by the rules. He does not abide by the laws. He is different. We have to stop him. Fight him. Weaken his resolve. Eliminate him. Stone him. Let he who is without sin cast the first stone.

Day and night
9 Jesus answered, Hath not the day twelve hours? He that walketh by day stumbleth not: for he seeth the light of this world. 10 But he that walketh by night stumbleth: for there is no light in him.

Day and night. Light is bright, clear, safe, positive, they say. Night is dark, dangerous, frightening, brutal, they say. I am a child of the night. Hiding, I need the protection of darkness. Need the late hours for secret rendezvous, awkward encounters, invisible love. A hidden life. Life in the closet. Masked. In the darkness. The day is what kills me. The day is my make-believe world, filled with the bright lights of lies and stories. I need the darkness to survive. But now I am up to my neck in darkness, and I realize, I also need the light.

Sleep and death
11 This he said, and after that he said to them: Lazarus our friend sleepeth, but I go that I may awake him. 12 Then said the disciples unto him, Lord, if he sleeps, things have turned for the better with him. 13 But Jesus spoke of his death: but they thought that he spoke of the rest of sleep.

Every sleep is a death. And every death is a sleep. Going to sleep when living is too exhausting. Retreat under the covers. Off into the darkness. I can barely stand brightness and light. When the lies become too much. This double life is too complicated, sleep is a blessing. Every sleep is a death. And every death is a sleep.

Go with him
14 Then Jesus said to them freely, Lazarus is dead; 15 and I am glad for your sakes that I have not been there, that ye may believe. But let us go to him! 16 Then Thomas, who is called the twin, said unto the other disciples, Let us go with him, that we may die with him.

Walk with him. Let us go with him. Through the night. Through obstacles. Through dangers. Together, not alone. Let us go with him. Without knowing the destination. Just with him. Live with him. Die with him. Not alone. In living. In dying. Not alone.

Mourning and comfort
17 Then Jesus came and found Lazarus already four days in the tomb. 18 Now Bethany was near Jerusalem, about fifteen stadia away. 19 Many had come to Martha and Mary to comfort them because of their brother. 20 Now when Martha heard that Jesus was coming, she went to meet him; but Mary remained sitting in the house.

We had no idea. If only we had known. We would have looked after him sooner. How tragic. Such a nice young man. We'd never have guessed. He's not like that. No, he looks so normal. It can't be. How could this happen? What will the parents think? What will the neighbors say? What did they do wrong? They didn't deserve this. This is the end.

Do you believe that?
21 Then Martha said to Jesus, "Lord, if you had been here, my brother would not have died. 22 But even now I know that whatever you ask of G*d, G*d will give you. 23 Jesus saith unto her, Thy brother shall rise again. 24 Martha says to him, I know that he will rise again at the resurrection on the last day. 25 Jesus says to her: I am the resurrection and the life. He that believeth in me, though he were dead, yet shall he live: 26 And whosoever liveth and believeth in me shall never die.

Do you believe that? Do you believe in life? Do you believe in being free? Free from a double life. Free from fear. Free to be who you are. No longer buried alive. No longer in a grave of lies. No longer in a grave of masks and entanglements. Free at last. Do you believe that?

Secretly
27 She saith unto him, Yea, Lord, I believe that thou art the Christ, the Son of G*d, which is come into the world. 28 And when she had said this, she went and called her sister Mary, and said unto her privily, The Master is here, and calleth thee.

Secretly, so that no one hears. Secretly, so that no one sees it, no one knows. A secret kiss. A secret different life. Secretly taking someone into your confidence. Finally saying something. Finally rising from the vault of lies and silence. A beginning. At last.

If only you had been there
29 When Mary heard this, she arose in haste and came to him. 30 Now Jesus had not yet come into the village, but was still where Martha had met him. 31 When those who were with her in the house and were comforting her saw that Mary got up in haste and went out, they followed her, thinking: She is going to the tomb to weep there. 32 When Mary therefore came to where Jesus was, and saw him, she fell at his feet, and said unto him, Lord, if thou hadst been here, my brother had not died.

If only you had been there. Maybe I would have been braver. Less isolated, less scared, less frozen, less beside myself. If only you had been there, I would have had more courage to stand up. Out of the tomb of lies. From the illusion of being protected by silence, by the darkness. From the life that is not mine. If only you had been there.

About the eyes
33 And when Jesus saw her weeping, and the Jews also weeping which came with her, he was moved in spirit, and trembled, 34 And said, Where have ye laid him? They said to him, Lord, come and see. 35 And Jesus' eyes went out.

It is through the eyes that tears come. Through the eyes, the boundaries between light and dark, clear and distorted, right and wrong, dead and alive, normal and abnormal become blurred. Through the eyes come the tears. Grief becomes visible. Everything flows, changes. At some point, nothing holds you back anymore. Through your eyes come the tears. About a life unlived, about opportunities missed, courage lost. It's through the eyes.

A stone
36 And the people said, Behold, how he loved him! 37 But some of them said: He opened the eyes of the blind man; could he not also make this man not die? 38 Then Jesus was angry again, and came to the sepulchre. And there was a cave, and a stone was before it. 39 Jesus saith, Take away the stone.

A stone lies on my chest. Blocking my life and my breathing. A stone blocks my way. Inside and outside. The stone: blocking my way, an obstacle, a wall. Keystone, cornerstone, building stone, kidney stone. The stone on my chest blocks my life. Lift it, the stone.

Come out!
39 Marta, the sister of the deceased, says to him: Lord, he stinketh already; for he hath lain four days. 40 Jesus saith unto her, Did I not say unto thee, If thou shalt believe, thou shalt see the glory of G*d? 41 Then they lifted away the stone. And Jesus lifted up his eyes, and said, Father, I thank thee that thou hast heard me. 42 I knew that thou hearest me always: but for the sake of the people that stand about, I said it, that they might believe that thou hast sent me. 43 When he had said this, he cried with a loud voice, Lazarus, come out.

Come out! Come out of your tomb! Come out of your hell! Come out of your petrification! Go on! Dare! Trust him! Listen to his voice! Come out! Don't be buried alive any longer. Live!

Unbind the bandages!
44 And the deceased came out bound with grave clothes on his feet and hands, and his face was covered with a facecloth. Jesus said to them: Unbind him and let him go.

Undo the bandages and let him go! Towards himself. Towards his life. Towards his love. Towards himself, just as he is. Without bindings. Without chains. Without a grave. Untie him and let him go. Let him live his own life. Without sin. Without hate and violence. Without shame. Without insecurity. Untie him and let him go! Let me go. Let us go. And suddenly you go. Shakily. Incredulous. Carefully. Unbound. Without shackles. Lazarus comes out. You come out. You allow yourself to go. Out of the tomb. You allow yourself to cry, to laugh, to rise. Resurrected to life.

2.2 Resonances

The story of burial and resurrection had a great impact on many of us. It took some time to listen to and absorb the different feelings expressed within the small groups and in the plenary sessions afterwards. For this purpose, I set up a "station at the tomb" and a "resurrection station in front of the empty tomb" in the large plenary hall. The stations were marked by name. Cloth, candles, various other symbols and blank-colored cards were placed at each station. The participants were asked to write keywords on the cards and place them at the respective stations. At two stations and at a third station "in between" they could stop and exchange ideas. Intense conversations followed. At the station at the grave, keywords like "frozen", "no lust for life", "buried", "imprisoned", "invisible", "burying feelings," "gagged," "the Bible kills," and others were left. At the resurrection station, terms like "finally free!", "coming out", "joyful", "alive and queer", "I'm leaving the church!", "without contempt and discrimination!", "love is love!", "never hide again!" could be found.

At the station "In-between" there were keywords like "I'm still searching", "Where is the exit?", "Can I really be like this?", "Caught between two stools", "I don't fit anywhere", "Longing for belonging!" and others. The cards were placed on plain packaging paper in the middle of the room and then used to create a colorful collage. Afterwards, each participant could choose one of the terms as a baseline to formulate a poem, a prayer or a psalm of lament. Finally, those who wanted to, recited their texts. It was a touching performance, as well as a queer-affirming and much-appreciated task that occupied some people for a long time, as I know from the individual conversations that followed.

In this case, the pastoral sermon served as the motivation for structured further processing of thoughts and feelings. As in the first example, the participants acted as temporary pastors for each other. Collegial discussion, empathy and compassion based on their own experiences became key components of these interactions. The sermon put something into words that, for some, had remained unspoken until then.

3 "Zacchaeus and the shame" – The story of the tax collector told from a queer perspective

3.1 Sermon

A biblical story in which feelings of shame are particularly apparent is the story of the tax collector Zacchaeus. It is found in Luke 19:1–10. I delivered this reflective sermon at an international queer conference of the European Forum of LGBTI+ Christian Groups.[28] Shame is a familiar theme for many queer people, thus this story especially resonates with them.

The tax collector

Zacchaeus was not respected by the people of his town Jericho, for he was a tax collector. People said he took advantage of his profession and acted fraudulently. When Jesus came to Jericho one day, Zacchaeus climbed a mulberry tree by the roadside and hid there.

The Bible text tells us that Zacchaeus was small in stature, hence he could see better from the tree. But his elevated hideout also gave him the opportunity to remain unseen by the inhabitants of the city and Jesus. Zacchaeus knew that people did not like him, he was ashamed of his profession and his self-esteem was nigh on non-existent. He preferred to remain hidden in the shadows and lived alone, unappreciated and disrespected.

Shame and feelings of inferiority

Many lesbian, gay, bisexual, trans*, inter* and queer people know this feeling. Unlike Zacchaeus, they do not have a dubious profession *per se,* nor have they done anything reprehensible. Yet many feel ashamed. Some are uncomfortable with the fact that they are lesbian, gay, bisexual, or trans*. This is because sexual diversity and non-binary gender identities are still considered controversial or shameful in society and in the church. In many religious circles, they are still far from being recognized. Others are still afraid to show who they love, or to reveal which gender identity they feel most comfortable with. Just like Zacchaeus, they struggle with shame and feelings of inferiority.

LGBTQI+ people experience being looked down upon, made fun of, or even attacked and ostracized on a daily basis. Deeply internalized homophobia or transphobia are widely felt additional challenges and pose a major problem especially for LGBTQI+ people from right-wing evangelical or very devout families. It is a sad fact that families,

---

28 The meditation is inspired by Rev. Wielie Elhorst from Amsterdam, who gave a talk on "Zacchaeus" at an international queer conference in 2019. First published in: Söderblom (2021c).

school classes, peer groups, or professional environments often convey to them that they are weird, strange, and don't belong. Some religious groups call them sinful or even condemn them. As a result, self-acceptance doesn't come easily.

Jesus is coming!
As Jesus passed by, he went directly to the mulberry tree where Zacchaeus was sitting, looked up, and said clearly, *"Zacchaeus, come down quickly, for I must stop at your house today!" (Luke 19:5b).*

Jesus wanted to come to his house the same day. What an announcement! The people in the crowd reacted angrily. Why did Jesus want to go to Zacchaeus' house? He was a sinner, a cheat, a cutthroat, a bad person, and a nuisance to them.

Amazement and joy
Zacchaeus, on the other hand, reacted with amazement and joy to Jesus' invitation. With renewed vigor, he jumped down from the tree and ran home. He wanted to prepare everything for Jesus' visit. It is noticeable that Jesus said nothing from then on until the end of the story. The only surviving sentence is the one that Jesus speaks at the end of the story:

"Today salvation has come to this house (of Zacchaeus, K. S.), because he, too, is a son of Abraham" (Luke 19:9).

Transformation
Jesus looked at Zacchaeus and spoke to him and that alone completely transformed him. He no longer hid, but jumped down from the tree and rejoiced. Jesus changed his life. He also affirmed to Zacchaeus that he belonged, even though he was unpopular and considered himself unworthy. Jesus vindicated him in front of everyone by calling him a "son of Abraham." Zacchaeus was also a citizen of Israel and a descendant of Abraham. It was common knowledge at the time that Abraham was the forefather of Israel and the recipient of G*d's blessing and G*d's promises – and it is important to take this into account.

Zacchaeus is one of them!
The people of Jericho did not like this. They were indignant and whispered behind his back, but they did not criticize Jesus aloud. Nor did they stop him from going to Zacchaeus. And Jesus did not let them stop him, neither. He had made it clear – no matter what Zacchaeus had done or not done, he had never been outside of G*d's covenant with Israel. Zacchaeus had an unpopular job, and he was not popular either. But he belonged, just like everyone else. Therefore, he should no longer be ashamed.

Today in a queer shared apartment
It would be exciting to see what would happen if Jesus came and visited the shared apartment of some LGBTQI+ people today. I imagine it would go something like this: The people around would be outraged.

Why does Jesus go to these strange dykes, faggots and trannies? What does he want there? They don't deserve him. He should come to us instead!

The queer shared apartment, on the other hand, would be in turmoil: They would be cleaning up, turning on music, cooking up something delicious to eat, and chilling a few bottles of wine and beer. They would be excited. Because a visit from such a significant person would clearly show them that, yes, we sometimes feel inferior and ashamed because many think we are strange or even sick. But we are worth just as much as everyone else. This Jesus sees us as we are, and accepts us. Jesus visits us, wants to eat and talk with us. Wow! How cool is that! Jesus does not consider us second-rate or sick or perverted. Let's get this party started!

Respect and recognize
Against all odds, Jesus rehabilitated Zacchaeus and made it clear that he, too, was a son of Abraham. Jesus' meal with Zacchaeus gave the latter a chance to feel seen. He felt appreciated, simply because Jesus was there. It helped him leave his shame behind and change his life, inwardly for himself and outwardly before others. Zacchaeus was seen and recognized by Jesus. This was a completely new and life-changing experience for him. He then promised to donate money to the poor, and to refund those he had defrauded.

Strengthening for body, mind and soul
Experiences of respect and recognition can also be life-changing and liberating for queer people. Of course, depending on your life story, it takes a long time to leave shame and insecurity behind. And it takes even longer to be proud of your life and accept yourself. For some, it is even a lifelong challenge. Others need continuous therapeutic support to achieve this.

But what is certain, is that when people are seen, taken seriously and recognized, their self-esteem is strengthened. Jesus described this as salvation for Zacchaeus' house. And he was right – being seen and accepted is healing. Sure, there is no guarantee this will happen and no magic potion to achieve it. But it helps to reduce shame and insecurity and strengthens individuals in body, mind and soul.

3.2 Resonances

Using questions for guidance, following the sermon, we talked about life situations in which individuals present had felt alone, marginalized or ashamed. Very different experiences were shared. Afterwards, we discussed how their respective stories continued. Were there people who stuck by them or who came alongside them, who took them seriously without judging them? Was there a "Jesus moment" in which they felt heard, even if others didn't hear them? Were they able to tell their story and did someone listen? In small groups, the participants shared their experiences and then fed back short examples of how they had escaped from lonely and/or shameful situations and who had helped them. This form of sharing based on the biblical story facilitated awareness of personal potential and of people who were there for them, and who had remained there for them, despite experiences of strangeness. The people in the group acted mindfully and considerately and in this way, became queer-affirming companions. This is another possibility of low-threshold queer-affirming pastoral care.

4 "Losing and finding again" – The story of the Prodigal Son told from a queer perspective

4.1 Sermon

People long for peace and reconciliation. But the reality is often quite different. Which is why it is all the more powerful when reconciliation succeeds. A biblical story that tells us about a situation like this is the story of the prodigal son. It is found in Luke 15:11–32. The trans* playwright Jo Clifford told me the story from her perspective some time ago (see Clifford 2019, pp. 16–18). I first wrote down the story for a morning talk on the radio station SWR 1 in December 2021 (Söderblom 2021b).

Going away to find yourself.
A father had two sons. At some point, one of the two sons knew that he was actually a daughter. Therefore, he went to the father, asked for forgiveness and explained that he could no longer be his son. The father could not accept this. He threw his son, who was actually a daughter, out of the house. The daughter went far away to another country. There she threw herself into life and took on every adventure. But she was not lucky: Soon her money ran out and she ended up on the street. She found work in a hotel kitchen. It was a tiring, dirty, and horribly paid job. She often thought that she was treated worse there than her father treated his animals. So she finally decided to return home and ask her father for forgiveness. Since she could no longer be his son, perhaps it was possible to work in his stables as a helping hand.

Return and reconcile

The story then took a quite unexpected turn of events: When her father saw her coming, he ran toward her and cradled her in his arms. He had missed her so much. And he had understood that she remained his child. He told his daughter to bathe and put on clean clothes. There was to be a great celebration.

When the party was already in full swing, the older son came back from the office. When he heard what was going on, he became angry: *"I have always been a good and obedient son to you,"* he said. *"And what did I get in return? But when this pervert comes home, he gets everything. That's not fair!"*

The father replied:

"It is true that you have always been a good son. I thank you for that. But my other son had lost his life and found herself again after a long journey. And now I have also found her again as a daughter. This is cause for celebration!" And that's exactly what they did.

4.2 Resonances

I received numerous responses to the radio broadcast by e-mail. Some people responded very negatively. They were outraged that I could spoil the biblical story in such a way. Other feedback had a more positive or grateful tone. There were parents of transgender youth, non-binary and trans* people who thanked me and underlined how beneficial it was to have a biblical story told from a queer perspective for once. They emphasized that they had never thought about looking at and telling the story from a trans* perspective before. Some of them felt encouraged to look at Bible stories from a queer perspective more often, and asked me for literature about it. A queer-affirming biblical hermeneutic can encourage queer people to steer their own path.

5 "Out of the Box!" – Beyond pigeonholes told from a queer perspective

5.1 Sermon

I wrote the reflective sermon for a service at a 2018 meeting of the mentoring program for queer and Christian activists from Eastern Europe in Tbilisi, Georgia.[29] It was a program offered by the European Forum of LGBTI+ Christian Groups, which paired twenty queer Christians from different European countries for two years. The entire group met three times during that time. A church service and daily devotions were also part of the program. The biblical text was Exodus 3:14.

---

29 I published the sermon meditation as part of a blog post in: Söderblom (2020a, p. 235 f.).

Drawers
I find myself in various drawers: large, small, high, deep, with corners and edges. Some with openings, others totally closed, without air and without light. Drawers everywhere.

Who am I?
A woman, daughter, sister, aunt, partner, a friend who loves a woman. A seeker, a doubting believer, a believing doubter, a queer pastor, counselor, professional theologian, passionate activist, a German, sports lover, bon vivant, over fifty …
    What do all these labels and terms say about me? I do not know.

Pressure
But what I do know is that I feel pressure, expectations, a huge weight on my shoulders. I try to live up to pigeonholes and categories. I try to meet expectations. And I feel inadequate, exhausted, small, ill-suited. I don't fit in.

I am here!
And when Moses saw the burning bush in the wilderness, he asked G*d:
    "What should I tell the people of Israel about who You are?"

And G*d answered:
"I am who I am! I am here and talking to you. I stay with you and bless you. I am with you whether you realize it or not. I will lead you out of slavery and oppression in Egypt and elsewhere. I am present and absent. I am here and there, near and far, understandable and tangible, unavailable and beyond human logic. I am the power of love and liberation. I am beyond categories, pigeonholes and human ideas."

And G*d continued to speak:
"And I say to you, you are made in my image.
My child, created and blessed by me.

I am who I am, beyond pigeonholes and labels.
And you are who you are, beyond pigeonholes and labels.
Worthy, unique and blessed. Each individual.
Without pigeonholes to fit or expectations to fulfill.
Just be who you are and follow your path. Because it's a lifelong journey."

And G*d continued:
"Go and tell the people in Israel and beyond. I am who I am.
And you are who you are.
*A child of G*d, wonderfully made, called to love*
and called to leave hatred, oppression and violence behind.
Encouraged to find your own talents and passions, strengthened by my love.
So that you can love yourself and your neighbors.
Now go in peace and leave the drawers behind!"

5.2 Resonances

On the day before the service we dealt with the norms, categories and pigeonholes that queer believers find themselves up against. Depending on background, context, denomination and piety milieu very different terms and pigeonholes came up. We proceeded to write these terms down on cardboard boxes and then constructed a wall out of them, symbolizing the walls in our heads, our hearts, and in the outside world and church environment. After the service the next day, we turned on loud music – "I am what I am" by Amanda Lear. While listening to the song, we removed the boxes from the wall, threw them back and forth, played with them, threw them away, returned them. In the end, the wall was gone and the boxes had become colorful permeable shapes that were no longer threatening, albeit still there. We continued to work with these structures afterwards, asking ourselves what queer people need in order to break down the walls of expectations and norms in their own minds and all around them. Encouragement in faith matters served as a resource, as did queer-affirming services and prayers.

Once again, the participants became pastors for each other. They listened to each other, conveyed understanding and compassion, and gathered ideas and strategies. The sermon served to strengthen group ties and pastoral support on the journey.

6 "You shall be a blessing!" – Blessings told from a queer perspective

6.1 Sermon

The Latin word for "to bless" is "benedicere." Literally translated that means saying good things, saying yes, wishing others well. Blessing relates to the whole life, including mind, heart and physical body, with every fiber of one's existence. And the story of Abraham and Sarah in Genesis 12:2b is precisely about that and for exactly that reason, it remains still relevant when it comes to the controversy regarding blessing same-sex couples. I preached this sermon at a morning service at the Protestant University Chaplaincy in Mainz.

"I will bless you!"

With this blessing, G*d addressed the insecure Abraham, encouraging him to leave his homeland and dare something new. In doing so, G*d promised:

"I will bless you!"

Abraham listened to G*d and opened himself up to being touched. The encouragement resonated in him and he told his wife Sarah about it. Together they dared to listen to G*d's voice and decided to trust G*d.

Departure

And so they consciously took the next steps. First, they had to say goodbye to their home, their family, their neighborhood, their parents' house, their culture, their language and their entire community – everything that had offered them support and protection, everything they had known until then.

G*d called Abraham and Sarah to leave their previous existence in Ur in Chaldea of Mesopotamia between the rivers Euphrates and Tigris and to embark on a journey into the unknown. They had no insurance policy, no compass to guide them, and could not be certain that everything would go well until they arrived in ... well, where, actually?

The only thing that bridged the gap between the familiar and the new was the words that Abraham had heard from G*d. I will bless you. I will bless you and with you, your clan. You will be well off, your will have land and descendants. This is what G*d promised in the first book of Moses (Genesis 12:1–3).

The pain of farewell and hope

They followed the way, with sadness and worry, uncertainty and hope in tow. How would the journey through the desert go? Would they stay healthy? Would they find enough food, survive challenges?

G*d's blessing was closely connected to the pain of farewell, but they dared to go anyway. They packed up their tents, their herd of cattle and whatever else they had and set out. Perhaps they'd had a farewell feast beforehand. Or maybe they left their home in a cloak-and-dagger operation. Either way, they opened themselves to the blessing that G*d had promised. They could have refused the invitation. They could have stayed put in the security of the family, the safety of the clan, and the familiar religious traditions. But they decided to set out and head toward the new. G*d's encouragement sounded in their hearts:

"I will bless you ...!"

For this blessing, they traveled far beyond their comfort zone into the freedom to which G*d was calling them. There were times when they were unsettled, when they were dithering, moaning, complaining and not seeing when, how and where they were supposed to arrive. They made mistakes, got lost, were hungry and thirsty, and cursed the moment they had left more than once.

Encouragement
But G*d's encouragement weighed heavier than their doubt. With every step they entered deeper into their relationship with G*d and Their living power to bless. Finally, they actually arrived in Canaan and built a new existence there. They had descendants, and they prospered. G*d's blessing passed from them to their descendants and eventually to all the peoples of the earth.

*G*d's Shalom*
Blessing is G*d's gift to us. With it, G*d sends the fullness of life to us: G*d's shalom. And that means peace, community and well-being as a holistic and collective basis of life.

In the biblical story, however, it is crucial that G*d's blessing to Abraham and Sarah has a second part:
"... and you shall be a blessing!"
I will bless you and you shall be a blessing, it says. Or simply: Become a blessing! To be a blessing, to become a blessing, that is about your whole existence. It is about receiving and passing on. And it is about doing. Acting responsibly and caringly in community, in partnership and for oneself. People are given the blessing of G*d in order to be able to pass it on. Thus, blessing is not bound to a specific function, but to everyday activities.

No second-class blessing
For G*d's blessing does not belong to people. Consequently, they cannot and must not abuse it to bless some and deny blessings to others, as the Vatican's Congregation for the Doctrine of the Faith did toward same-sex couples in March 2021. Second-class blessings do not exist.

Blessing is a promise and G*d's gift to the people. Whether and how G*d's blessing works is not in human hands. People can, however, trust in the effectiveness of the blessing, receive it and pass it on to others.

#LoveWins
In this respect, the #LiebeGewinnt (#LoveWins) campaign that took place in numerous Catholic parishes on May 10, 2021 was ecclesiastically and theologically symbolic, and has been repeated every year ever since. But above all, it was also a deeply human one. On that day, blessing services were held in over one hundred Catholic churches in Germany. I was present at the blessing ser-

vice of the Catholic University Chaplaincy (KHG) in Mainz. Individuals and couples were blessed, regardless of marital status, sexual orientation or gender identity. We were wished good things: physically, spiritually, mentally. It was good for everyone.

It was a powerful riposte to the statement of the Congregation of Faith that same-sex couples may not be blessed. For G*d's blessing cannot be ruled over. It does not belong to cardinals, bishops or priests. The subject of every act of blessing is G*d Themselves.

Receive blessing and become a blessing
Strengthened by G*d's blessing, people can actively ensure that they themselves become a blessing to others. There are many ways in which people pass on blessings – entertaining loving thoughts about a person; placing a hand on a person's head or shoulder and speaking a kind word; a gesture of blessing, a prayer of blessing. A word of blessing can encourage and strengthen people today just as it did Abraham and Sarah back then. And that is so important when it comes to setting out and daring to do something new.

So may G*d's blessing be with us all! Amen.

6.2 Resonances
After each morning service at the Protestant University Chaplaincy, we bake pancakes, drink coffee, and swap ideas. That morning our minds were still occupied with "blessings." Some students had also been present at the blessing service of the Catholic University Chaplaincy and reported how beautiful it had been to see everyone being blessed, regardless of the kind of relationship involved. It had been good for them, they said. Others agreed, emphasizing that it was important for them to hear that blessings come from G*d and are passed on by people. They were relieved that the act of blessing was not to be used as weapon against people, but rather as encouragement to wish people well. They wanted to remember this in the future and do it themselves. The power of blessing was meaningful to all present. With the story of Abraham and Sarah, they could now better source and understand this power from a biblical perspective. At the end of the conversation, one student reiterated that it was important for everyone to be blessed, not just some. This insight was decisive for the group that morning, and after breakfast they left in a happy state of mind, strengthened in body, mind and soul.

7 "Jacob, Rachel, Leah & Co." – Family dispute in the house of Jacob told from a queer perspective

7.1 Sermon

I preached this sermon on 11th November 2020 at the University Chaplaincy in Mainz as part of the opening service on the semester theme "We are Family". In the service I was also introduced as a university pastor to the ESG in Mainz. The biblical text is based on Genesis 25–48. In German the stanzas rhyme.

I

Hey Jacob, your family was complicated from the beginning.
Your problem was the blessing that started it all.
You tricked father Isaac and brother Esau,
With fur on your skin and with Mother Rebekah,
you tricked them darn good, but it all came at a price.
You had to get the f... out

Refrain
Family, family, what does it mean?
Every experience gives the word a different tone.
People are married, divorced, widowed, single,
with and without children, lesbian, gay, colorful, queer, far away and close by.
No matter how families live, G*d is there.
Care and respect are important, otherwise it's over.

II

In Canaan, your uncle Laban took you in.
You worked hard and were not in a good mood at all.
You fell in love with Rachel. After seven years you wanted to marry. But Laban explained:
First you have to marry Leah,
she was the older of the two women.
Seven years later, you were finally allowed to kiss Rachel as well.
The time in between was one of longing and hard work.

III
12 boys you have fathered with four women.
Polygamous conditions, your head was bowed.
You must have had girls, too.
But they counted for little, I know today with trepidation.
Besides, there were maids and servants, flocks of sheep and goats.
Your household was large and hard to defeat.

Refrain
Family, family, what does it mean?
Every experience gives the word a different tone.
People are married, divorced, widowed, single, with and without children,
lesbian, gay, colorful, queer, far away and close by.
*No matter how families live, G*d is there.*
Care and respect are important, otherwise it's over.

IV
Then you set off again for your homeland, the way was long.
And you knew you would meet Esau again.
You were so sorry for the deception.
On the bank of the Jabbok you wrestled with G*d at night.
In your misery you needed his blessing.
Because only with G*d's blessing could you meet Esau again.
You were afraid of him, so G*d should bless you.

V
So it came to pass the next day, you were reconciled.
Esau forgave you, he did not mock you.
You had your extended family, with four wives, twelve sons, herds and cattle.
Don't tell me your family was a role model, no way, never!
Of the sons, Joseph was your favorite, you made it clear.
The other sons were jealous, and it did not end well.
Joseph told stories, he dreamed and sang,
the others worked in the field and their envy was loud.

Refrain
Family, family, what does it mean?
Every experience gives the word a different tone.
People are married, divorced, widowed, alone,
with and without children, lesbian, gay, colorful, queer, far away and close by.
No matter how families live, G*d is there.
Care and respect are important, otherwise it's over.

VI
Only to Joseph you gave a special dress.
This stirred up hatred among the brothers and their envy.
Joseph wore the dress with pride and pleasure,
the others watching him with annoyance growing in their hearts.
Then Joseph dreamed dreams of content unheard-of.
He was the boss and everyone stopped and bowed down.
No wonder the others were angry, and they made a plan.

VII
One day in the field, the time had come.
The brothers grabbed Joseph, threw him into the well, no one saw him far and wide.
They finally sold him to a merchant of a caravan.
They told the father that Joseph was dead, and he mourned, poor man.

Refrain
Family, family, what does it mean?
Every experience gives the word a different tone.
People are married, divorced, widowed, alone,
with and without children, lesbian, gay, colorful, queer, far away and close by.
No matter how families live, G*d is there.
Care and respect are important, otherwise it's over.

VIII
Hey Jacob, your family was complicated from the beginning.
Now it was your son Joseph's turn to have problems.
In Egypt he was thrown into a dungeon.
For with Potiphar's wife he kept a low profile.
He was different from the others, he did not want to cheat.
He wanted to observe, to dream. He didn't care about the lies.

IX
In prison, he had to interpret many a dream.
Word got around – even among the Pharaoh's people.
He was called to advise Pharaoh.
They had indeed come to the right man.
Joseph advised them to stockpile and that should save them.
For seven years of hunger came after seven fat years.
Joseph had advised Pharaoh wisely.
Later the Pharaoh prided himself with his quotes.

Refrain
Family, family, what does it mean?
Every experience gives the word a different tone.
People are married, divorced, widowed, alone,
with and without children, lesbian, gay, colorful, queer, far away and close by.
No matter how families live, G*d is there.
Care and respect are important, otherwise it's over.

X
Thus the prisoner became the second man in the state.
And his brothers ended up with Joseph, they had made their own beds.
They had come from Israel to Egypt because of the famine.
They were shocked and still dazed by the hardship.
Hence they did not recognize Joseph, it had been too long.
Joseph, though, recognized his brothers immediately. It was not difficult for him.

XI
He was happy to see them again in spite of everything.
He asked for the youngest brother Benjamin and let them go.
They returned with Benjamin and father Jacob.
They were given food and they were lucky
that Joseph wanted to reconcile with them.
Hatred and revenge did not swallowed them up.

Refrain
Family, family, what does it mean?
Every experience gives the word a different tone.
People are married, divorced, widowed, alone,
with and without children, lesbian, gay, colorful, queer, far away and close by.
No matter how families live, G*d is there.
Care and respect are important, otherwise it's over.

XII
So the family reunited in Egypt.
They celebrated reconciliation and sang old songs.
The family of Jacob, Rachel, Leah and the others –
their story was complicated, quarrelsome and without flow.
But Joseph had survived the hatred.
He was smart and different and very eager.
As a man, not to act in a typically masculine way.
Instead, he walked around in a dress and was a master of negotiation.
Despite all the dangers, G*d's blessing was upon Joseph.
Because of a ruse, his father had enjoyed that too – on all his journeys.

XIII
The family of Jacob, Rachel, Leah and Co.
It remained complicated, and let's put it this way:
History shows what is true to this day:
Families are diverse and more diverse than the norm allows for.
Even in the Bible, they were a colorful bunch.
It is not worth running away from the realization.
That's why I say it once more in conclusion,
so that all shall know, without confusion:

Refrain
Family, family, what does it mean?
Every experience gives the word a different tone.
People are married, divorced, widowed, alone,
with and without children, lesbian, gay, colorful, queer, far away and at home.
No matter how families live, G*d is there.
Care and respect are important, otherwise it's over. Amen

7.2 Resonances

After the service we managed to raise our glasses in a way that conformed to the hygiene measures in place at the time. We also found time to gather around the fireplace, where St. Martin's fire shone brightly. Some students came up to me and thanked me for the sermon. Some of them wanted to have a written version of the sermon so that they could read the text again.

"It was so good to hear that in the Bible, too, everything was already colorful and diverse and not as uniform as the pastor in my home parish used to preach to us!" said one student.

Another chimed in: *"Jacob, Rachel and the others were real soap stars. I didn't know there were stories like that in the Bible!"*

"Yes, they're much more modern than I thought," said a third.

Refilling their glasses, some said it also depended on who read and told the stories, to avoid run-of-the-mill interpretations. With a smile, they emphasized that it was nice that queer perspectives had a place in the sermon preached by the Protestant University Chaplain.

8 Conclusions

When queer-affirming pastoral preaching is done, unusual interpretations will emerge. Biblical stories are related to queer life stories and biblical stories are read in a queer way, so that they become relevant for queer Christians and for others as well. Unlike pastoral conversations, queer-affirming sermon reflections can offer meanings that do not require direct commentary or discussion. Listeners or re-readers are allowed to let the content sink in and digest it. Do they have questions, comments, or other reactions? Then they can write to the preacher or ask questions through other media channels. Queer-affirming pastoral sermons bridge the gap between biblical stories and real-life contexts and illuminate them from a queer perspective. Narrative texts and biographical storytelling are just as suitable for this type of sermon as meditations, poems, or literary contributions. I have given some examples of these in this chapter. The impact of the sermons is even more profound, though, if there is time after the services or during devotions for follow-up discussions, or for work in small groups. Confidential discussions with others and/or with the preacher may increase the meaningfulness of the message, and may lead to further reactions and comments which often relate to everyday experiences and individual life situations. The participants become queer-affirming companions and counselors for each other.

In this phase, life stories and faith stories can illuminate and interact with one another, creating new contexts and meanings. This form of interpretive work, oscillating between text and context, is fruitful for queer-affirming pastoral care. It includes the perspectives and voices of those who are familiar with the subject areas from their own experience or have something to say about them. This creates face to face participation, compassion, and solidarity among all involved. And it creates added value in terms of content and theology, which is also significant with relation to pastoral care.

INTERPRETATION

VIII Queer-affirming pastoral theology of diversity

1 Queer-affirming pastoral care – Requirements for the pastoral caregiver

The case studies I have presented, alongside their evaluation, show that the role of the pastoral caregiver plays a decisive and meaningful role in queer-affirming pastoral care. If pastors are sensitive and open to queer issues, this will come across in their attitudes and actions. Respect, understanding, and openness to the particular challenges of queer people make it possible to create a queer-friendly environment. This allows confidential spaces to emerge in which suffering, pain and experiences of conflict find just as much room, as experiences of joy and hope, and a longing for personal transformation.

Queer pastors have the advantage of being familiar with queer issues and challenges from their own experience. Therefore, they are usually able to meet those seeking queer pastoral care on a level playing field, and express a deeper sense of sympathy and empathy. This makes it possible for queer care seekers to open up, for trust to be built and for their concerns to be heard, discussed and resolved. Queer pastors can help build bridges and to finally leave behind the chasms in the complicated relationship between being Christian and queer.

Pastoral care should always be queer-affirming

Being a queer-friendly pastor and at the same time being heterosexual and cisgender (see glossary) are not mutually exclusive when it comes to providing professional pastoral support. In principle, every act of pastoral care should be queer-affirming. This means that pastors should always anticipate that people seeking pastoral care may be queer, or may have a differing gender identity from the one they expect, or may approach them with questions about queer issues.

The decisive factor here is a professional attitude which ensures that seekers of pastoral care are unreservedly recognized for who they are. Only if these basic rights are upheld, can meaningful dialogue take place and take shape between pastoral care giver and care-seeker.

In any case, queer-friendly counselors need to maintain a balance between closeness and distance, empathy and role reflection, understanding and curious inquiry. Of course, this does not only apply to queer issues, but in a queer context it is vital. And this is also why a certain degree of self-revelation, i.e. an appropriate openness and honesty of the chaplains with regard to their own experiences on the topic, is helpful. Therefore, regular reflection on one's own role and personal convictions with regard to queer issues is necessary.

Self-reflection

Counselors should be aware of their own prejudices and reservations about queer people. And they should also be aware of the fact that personal pain and trigger points, transferences and projections can influence their pastoral work.

In addition, queer-affirming chaplains need to recognize that queer people are at an increased risk of experiencing minority stress due to exclusion and other experiences of discrimination. They need to know that in their professional careers, queer people often feel the need to lead a double life, or may experience glass ceilings and social marginalization. They also need to be aware that LGBTQI + persons have often experienced exclusion and devaluation, especially in church settings, and therefore react suspiciously to offers of church support. They have to consider that minority stress makes people more susceptible to addictive substance use, self-hatred and/or auto-aggressive behavior.

In this respect, queer-affirming pastoral care entails acquiring information on these topics and developing a personal position on them. They should regularly review their attitude and behavior in supervision and in discussions with colleagues. This way, queer-affirming pastoral care work can increase in depth and be strengthened over time.

2 Queer-affirming pastoral care – Interpreting life in light of biblical stories

In all of the case studies, it was important for the seekers of pastoral care to be able to tell smaller or larger excerpts of their life stories. This allowed them to express their personal view of their lives. They experienced being listened to and non-devaluation of their viewpoints.

In pastoral counseling, life story work is a central building block (see also Weiß 2011, pp. 50–54), because every life story is unique, precious and identity-forming. It contains everything that people have experienced, suffered and stored in body and soul. At the same time, every life story told serves as an interpretive system through which people communicate with others and, in the best-case scenario, create meaningful connections. Queer people, however, often experience exactly the opposite. When they talk about their experiences and longings with regard to romantic relationships, sexuality or gender identity, they often experience resistance, incomprehension or alienation. Others reacting with doubt or aggression prevent queer people from experiencing understanding and sympathy when sharing intimate information about themselves. This leads to many of them not communicating anything about themselves at all, using codes to speak to one another in public, and/or leading a double life.

When queer-affirming counselors listen with interest and sympathy while queer people talk about their lives, this builds trust. When people feel taken seriously, new layers of meaning and interpretations can emerge. In this respect, queer-affirming pastoral care is always also about respectfully processing the life stories of queer people. Scenes from the individual´s life story are shared, and these can be reinterpreted within the context of their spiritual journey. This is a vital process in terms of coming to terms with one's back story.

When people feel respected and accepted, they also gain the courage to address hurt, suffering, and disappointment. Tears can flow and a hardened heart can mellow. Painful experiences and suffering need to be heard and understood. Then in time, the pain may subside or be transformed into a new understanding or experience. Scriptures, prayers or lines from psalms can play an important role in this process.

Queer-affirming pastoral care in the context of ceremonial services and sermons

The case studies in Chapter VI have shown that supportive queer-affirming pastoral care is significant in the context of ceremonial services. When blessing services for same-sex couples, naming ceremonies for trans* and non-binary persons, or funeral services for queer persons, are prepared and conducted, fragments of the life story and their interpretation are important components of pastoral support. The case studies in Chapter III also showed that it is helpful when personal challenges and crises can be linked to biblical stories. Indeed, it can be enormously valuable for queer people of faith to recognize themes from their life stories in biblical stories. The response to queer re-readings of biblical texts in my case studies demonstrates this powerfully. Queer-affirming Bible studies underline that people struggled with G*d in biblical times as well, despite very different life circumstances and contexts. They experienced that G*d was there and stayed close to people, especially in times of crisis and when people are at breaking point. Those who have primarily experienced devaluation and threats of hell and damnation in church or religious circles will gratefully receive G*d's encouragement in Scripture. For many, the permission to relate Scripture to one's own life story is a completely new experience. Biblical stories that are not imposed on people with missionary zeal, but offered as an aid to understand one's own life story, broaden horizons and open up new perspectives. In this sense, a queer biblical hermeneutic can become a key facet of queer-affirming pastoral care. In Chapter VII, I was able to capture concrete moments of realization that took place and were explored in small groups and during follow-up discussions after queer-affirming sermons.

For this reason, it is helpful if pastors have a selection of biblical stories that can be told from a queer perspective. It is equally important to know and be able to contextualize the content of the "clobber passages." The ability to be able to situate and explain biblical texts remains high, as some of the case studies have shown.

3 Queer-affirming pastoral care – Reciprocal relational events

Relationships are a basic dimension of life. People are dependent on them. Over the course of their lives, however, many queer people have experienced relationships breaking down when they came out as queer. For this reason, forming relationships and meeting people where they are at is a central task of pastoral care. People are accepted just as they are, regardless of skin color, background, physical ability, sexual orientation or gender identity. A safe space for conversation helps to build and try out respectful relationships. By means of role plays and practice conversations, individuals can prepare for situations in everyday life. Queer-affirming counseling sessions make it possible to discover one's own self-worth again in a safe space and to try out attitudes and express feelings which may then also be put into practice beyond the counseling session. For this to happen, a confidential relationship devoid of fear is necessary, which needs to be built up carefully. Protected spaces and pastoral confidentiality are central pillars, especially in queer-affirming pastoral care, in order to foster trust and promote openness.

But not every counseling session is successful. Misunderstandings, difficult environments, disagreements, content-related or even non-verbal factors can prevent a constructive pastoral care relationship. Even a queer-affirming attitude cannot always prevent this from happening.

4 Queer-affirming pastoral care – Activating personal strengths

Queer pastoral care seekers are unreservedly and without advance consideration regarded as images of G*d, just as any other seekers of counseling are. Their dignity is respected and will not be questioned. This means that the concerns of the other person are listened to openly and attentively in the counseling session. Together, the pastoral care giver and receiver will then work out what the conversation will be about. Time, place, and structure of the counseling sessions are agreed upon and protected. The limits of the counseling session are also clarified. People seeking advice who are also dealing with severe psychological problems or trauma are referred to psychotherapists or to appropriate specialized counseling centers. Trans* people with medical, legal and psychological questions need professional support with access to the appropriate expertise. This requires knowledge of the various counseling services in the region, good networking with the queer community and confidential cooperation when appropriate.

In pastoral counseling, no prescriptions for action are given. Instead, pastoral counselors offer support in a counseling process in which those seeking advice can discern their personal strengths and limitations, and discuss what the next steps could be. Therefore, the usual quality standards for responsibly conducted pastoral care and counseling sessions are adhered to.

The existing resources of the person seeking pastoral care are then reflected upon, with a view to changing the individual's current situation. The aim is to strengthen and encourage those seeking counseling to tap into their own abilities and not see their queerness as a deficit or flaw. In the case studies it became clear how liberating it was for the participants to see that their queerness was seen as something that has its own specific challenges, but which also leads to opportunities and possibilities. Those who have, or who are open to acquiring these skills, will be able to provide valuable shelter for queer people. For some queer people, this may even open up encouraging and empowering experiences in a church context.

Queer-affirming pastoral care and counseling work therefore makes an important contribution to the resources available to queer people, who often still experience themselves as inferior and unequal, especially in a church context.

5 Queer-affirming pastoral care – Language school for self-worth and social action

"I just can't find words for what I'm feeling and experiencing. It's like a big empty room that I can't access!" (J.)

Queer-affirming counseling can be seen as a language school, which creates liberating images, symbols and words that help the queer person relate experiences without fear and shame. Feelings such as pain, sadness or despair can be expressed in a safe, supportive environment. For this to take place, pastors should be compassionate and express solidarity. They should treat the queer person as an equal, instead of patronizing them or objectifying them in the act of compassion (see Kremer 2016, p. 183 f.).

Symbols, rituals, and acts of blessing can open up experiential spaces on a non-verbal level and facilitate a reinterpretation of past hurts and difficult life issues.

Queer-affirming pastoral care also links painful life experiences with social developments and structural challenges. This way, personal experiences of suffering are placed in a larger context and are no longer labelled as personal failures. In this sense, queer-affirming counseling helps to recognize and analyze discriminatory attitudes, values, norms and attributions. Queer people can then find words to see and analyze their personal situation in the context of socio-political environmental conditions. In this way, they are empowered and strengthened to understand their everyday experiences not as personal failures, but as examples of homo- and trans-hostility or collective persecution. In this respect queer-affirming pastoral care is also prophetic pastoral care. Its goal is to end injustice and discrimination and to enable socio-political transformation that guarantees justice and equality for all.

To achieve this goal, it is helpful if queer-affirming care is supported by other queer-affirming services. This can include queer-theological devotions, pride services, queer Bible studies, blessing services and weddings for same-sex couples, naming celebrations for trans* people, services for rainbow families and queer refugees, and other queer-affirming events.

Collaborations with queer self-help groups, other queer-affirming institutions, political groups and NGOs are also important. This is the only way to address the problems and challenges of queer people, not only on a personal but also on a socio-political level, and to improve their legal situation.

Lack of resources and limitations

However, a queer-affirming language school also has its limitations. Pastoral conversations remain open-ended in their course and impact. A biblical story or prayer does not fit every situation. Appropriate words, gestures or symbols cannot be found for every topic. Failure and unsuccessful conversations are part of everyday pastoral care. Pastors must be able to endure them and continue to work with them. They live in the hope that what they do is empowering and helpful, but there are no guarantees. It is not possible to control the impact of pastoral care. It has to be faithfully trusted to the power of the Holy Spirit.

A pastor should also work to the limitations of their professional remit. In the case of severely traumatized or psychologically ill people, pastors act professionally when they refer such individuals to therapeutic specialists, specialized counseling institutions or trauma specialists, whilst remaining in contact.

In the above situation, queer-affirming pastoral care may function as a kind of emergency pastoral care or crisis intervention between listening to the concern and referral to specialists. The behavior of the pastor is more direct and structured than in an open counseling conversation. Clear instructions are given, if necessary. Frameworks and rules are provided and referrals to appropriate specialists are offered (see Kremer 2016).

Another area in which boundaries should be respected for queer-affirming pastoral care are specific issues regarding trans* and intersex persons. Trans* people need legal and psychological counseling, medical advice and support, which require specific expertise. The German Society for Transidentity and Intersexuality (dgti*) or similar counseling institutions are important collaborative networks for this.[30] Queer-affirming pastoral care can offer assistance with religious questions, but cannot replace legal and medical expertise or therapeutic counseling.

6 Queer-affirming pastoral care – An innovative driver for welcoming and inclusive congregations

Perceiving, listening, and not judging are key competencies not only for pastors but overall for welcoming and inclusive communities. "This is how it has always been done" cannot be the default position here, as little can be taken for granted in a queer context. People and circumstances cannot be pigeonholed. Instead, unique and surprising facts can be brought to the table, when we keep an open mind. Active people of faith do not hide behind church doors, but go

---

30 See some examples of international queer-affirming religious networks at the end of this book.

out into their everyday worlds and meet others. And in so doing, they find that faith, spirituality, queerness and a commitment to equality do not contradict each other. On the contrary, they belong together.[31] New paths can be taken where there is room for creativity and experimentation (see Hartmann/Knieling 2016 on this, especially pp. 200–207). This way, queer people are seen as subjects and experts of their life stories and not only as objects of therapy and social work. This is a vital change of perspective (see Söderblom 2020a, p. 146f.).

I am convinced that dealing with queer and other minorities serves as a litmus test of how the church deals with those who are different for whatever reason, and whether dynamic and inclusive participation can thrive in a church context. The most important experience to note here is that when people inside and outside the church come together as equals and respect each other, they have fun together. They laugh and cry, talk and listen, pray and call out to G*d, praise and dance, mourn and celebrate. They form storytelling communities and share energy and hope for change. And they experience that they are not alone! Isn't that what church is all about?

7 Queer-affirming pastoral theology of diversity – Life-oriented, creative and transformative

From a queer-theological perspective, it is necessary to locate pastoral care and pastoral theological discourses within the various identity strands and their intersectional links, in order to adequately reflect the pluralistic lives of those seeking pastoral care. In such multi-systemic analytical perspectives, however, the limitations of heteronormativity and binary gender identities have so far been mostly ignored or only marginally considered. In this respect, queer-affirming research perspectives in pastoral theology add depth to these complex requirements. Queer-affirming theological approaches demonstrate how the consequences of heteronormativity and binary gender constructs reveal themselves in the life stories of queer people. Queer people struggle with reservations about them and grapple with religiously legitimized views that cast them as deficient or sinful beings. All of these issues can come up in pastoral conversations and it is necessary to further reflect and work on these topics pastorally and theologically.

---

31 Nadia Bolz-Weber reports this experience in her congregation of "All Sinners and Saints" (see Bolz-Weber 2016).

Such forms of analysis, reconstruction and changes in practice for pastoral theology represent a work in process, which by definition remains unfinished. In this respect, such processes are not only reconstructive and reflexive, but also actively orientated toward change and innovative implementation.

In this way, processes of perception and analysis already play an active part in the further development of a queer-affirming pastoral theology of diversity. They offer the advantage of giving perspective to life in all its diversity. They give language to diverse gender identities and sexualities, which can be topics in pastoral care conversations. They serve as motivation for personal development, for living together and for responsible behaviors beyond heteronormative and binary concepts. Finally, other differences with regard to background, skin color, age, culture, physical ability and religion are not ignored, but actively discussed in theological and pastoral discussions by reflecting on how we deal with foreignness and difference.

Queer-affirming knowledge and formation

Approaches to queer theologies involve reflections on diverse sexualities and gender identities in relation to theological and pastoral issues. These findings can be analyzed together with all other aspects of diversity in terms of their intersectional connections, with the aim of sensitizing people to the life situations of LGBTQI+ people. By making discrimination visible, its mechanisms can be explored methodically. For this purpose, a curriculum should be developed which offers bespoke modules and workshops on discrimination-free and queer-affirming pastoral care and counseling work in the context of pastoral care training.

A queer-affirming knowledge and training culture acts as a means of prevention as it prevents physical and psychological violence based on prejudice and makes social diversity visible. It delivers knowledge-based competencies aimed at changing attitudes and combatting persecution. It encourages people to deal with their sexual orientation and gender identity with confidence.

Furthermore, aspects of queer theologies show that justice, sensitivity and empathy towards sexual and other minorities are necessary. At the same time, they are an invitation to practice sensitivity to difference and acceptance of ambiguity. After all, people are different and move in very different worlds, contexts and value systems. The prerequisite for this is that differences are neither played off against each other, nor standardized, but rather accepted or even welcomed.

In this sense, the consideration of such queer-theological topics makes an invaluable contribution to a queer-affirming pastoral theology of diversity. Their insights should be integrated into theological education as mandatory. The same goes for further education and continued learning in the field of pastoral care. Theology and churches should no longer be part of the problem, but become part of the solution.

Glossary

Note: For the *italicized* terms I use the definitions of the Lesbian and Gay Association of Germany (LSVD) in its document on the self-determination law for trans* people (LSVD 2022).

CIS
The term "cis," short for "cisgender" refers to all individuals who identify with the gender they were assigned at birth.

COMING-OUT
"Coming out" describes the self-determined process of telling others about one's sexual orientation or gender identity. A distinction can be made between internal coming-out, i.e. becoming aware of oneself, and external coming-out, i.e. communicating one's identity to others.

DISCRIMINATION
Discrimination is the disadvantaging of a person or group on the basis of individual characteristics. Discrimination takes place in all areas of society. Discriminatory exclusion and disadvantage has in many cases developed over decades and centuries. Legal protection against discrimination is provided by the General Equal Treatment Act (AGG) and Article 3 of the Basic Law of the Federal Republic of Germany.

DIVERSE
Collective term for all those who do not perceive and live their gender identity as male or female.

ASTERISK*
Addendum used in words to include people living with non-binary gender identities (e.g. trans* or inter*). It is also used to make professions or definitions in German gender inclusive (e.g., pastors).

GENDER IDENTITY
Gender identity describes the gender to which a person feels a deep sense of belonging. This may differ from or coincide with the gender assigned at birth.

GENDER MARKER/MARITAL STATUS
In the civil status register, every child is assigned a gender at birth. This gender marker (female, male, diverse or open) can either be changed via § 45b of the Civil Status Act or the TSG (transsexual act), depending on the change desired.

G*D
Designation for God. It clarifies that the name of G*d is not pronounced in Hebrew and the vowels in the name of G*d are not written. This spelling marks the fact that G*d is beyond all human classification systems and attributions and eludes all categorizations – which is why I use this spelling. For the same reason I use the pronouns they, them, themselves for G*d.

HOMO-HOSTILITY
Homo-hostility is the term used to describe prejudice, hatred and violence against lesbian, gay and bisexual people. This term replaces "homophobia" to make clear that it is not about an irrational fear, but about discriminatory attitudes, behaviors and structures.

INTER*
Inter* or intersex people are people who were born with bodies that do not or only partially correspond with the common notions of "male" or "female" bodies. Inter* people, like all people, can identify as "male", "female", "trans*", "non-binary" or even identify exclusively as "inter*".

LGBTQI+
Lesbian, gay, bisexual, trans*, queer, inter* people. The plus indicates other unnamed forms of desire, (a-)sexualities and gender identities.

NON-BINARY
"Non-binary" is an umbrella term to describe people who locate themselves beyond, outside of, or between the assumed binary genders (female and male). Some non-binary people also see themselves as trans*, others as exclusively non-binary.

QUEER
Queer is an English derogatory term for lesbian, gay, bisexual, trans*, and inter* (LGBTQI+) people. Since the 1980s, the continuous use of the term in queer activism has transformed it into a creative and performative resource by LGBTQI+ persons and has been used as a self-description ever since. On a theoretical level,

the term "queer" provides a critical analytical term juxtaposed to heteronormative sexualities and binary gender identities. Queer is also often used as an umbrella term for LGBTQI+ persons.

SELF-DETERMINATION ACT
The passing of a self-determination law would allow trans*, inter*, and non-binary individuals to change first names and affirmed gender by making a declaration to the registrar's office.

TRANS*
"Trans*" is an umbrella term for all people who do not, or only partially identify, with the gender they were assigned at birth. This includes, for example, people who identify as transgender. Many non-binary individuals may also identify with the term "trans*."

TRANS-HOSTILITY
Trans-hostility is the term used to describe prejudice, hatred and violence against trans* people. This term replaces "transphobia" to make clear that it is not about an irrational fear, but about discriminatory attitudes, behaviors and structures.

TRANSGENDER
When a person's identity gender differs from the gender that was assigned at birth, the term "transgender" or "trans-identity" is used to describe that situation. These terms replace more pathological terms of foreign origin, such as "transsexuality" or "transsexualism" and also make it clear that it is about gender identity and not sexual orientation.

TRANSITION
After an inner coming out, many trans* persons start a process of transition in which they approach life in a new gender role by choosing a new first name or form of address (social transition), by officially changing their first name and affirmed gender (legal transition), or by hormone therapy and surgery (medical transition). It is an individual decision whether to take these steps and in what order.

TSG
The "Transsexuellengesetz" (TSG/Transsexual Act) of 1980 regulates the process of changing the name and affirmed gender of trans* people. The law has been criticized for decades because it is seen to violate fundamental rights. In 2022,

the introduction of a self-determination law was set in train (the key features of the self-determination law of the Federal Ministry for Family Affairs, Senior Citizens, Women and Youth in cooperation with the Federal Ministry of Justice have been available since June 2022. Further progress of the Act has been postponed several times since. In November 2023, the Act had its first reading in the German Bundestag. Its introduction has now been announced for November 2024). Due to largely unregulated public discussions of the Act over multiple media platforms, many passages have since been added to the original draft that are deemed highly problematic by all trans* advocacy groups in Germany.

(Self-)reflection questions for queer-affirming pastoral care[32]

1 Personal

- Which gender roles stereotypes shape my life and how do I view myself as female, male, non-binary or queer?
- Am I clear that pastoral care seekers may or may not be heterosexual and/or non-binary?
- By which pronouns do I want to be addressed?
- Do I ask pastoral care seekers what pronouns they would like to be addressed by?
- Which concepts of female, male and queer are positive for me and which are negative?
- Do I deal with my own prejudices, reservations and trigger points around other lifestyles, family types and gender identities than my own? What can I learn from this?
- Am I aware that I am also perceived by pastoral care seekers as a female/male/non-binary/queer role model? How do I deal with this?
- Do I know how to behave when people seeking pastoral care approach me about issues relating to different sexual orientations and/or gender identities?
- Am I aware that queer pastoral care seekers have often experienced marginalization, slander, and minority stress, and that biblical and theological language is often used to devalue or even as an act of violence? What does this mean for me and my work?
- Do I know any Bible stories that can be read from a queer perspective?
- Do I know the so-called "Clobber Passages" and what do I say about them when asked?

2 Structural

- Does my pastoral work contribute to making religious places, congregations or church institutions a place where those seeking pastoral care can feel safe from discrimination based on their sexual orientation and/or gender identity?
- Is it clear to those seeking pastoral care in my parish/church organization that we strive for equality of all sexualities and gender identities in church communities? How is this recognizable?

---

[32] Further reflective questions and guidelines on queer-affirming attitudes and behaviors (cultural, structural, practical) especially in school and religious education can be found in Pithan/Söderblom/Uppenkamp (2019).

- Does my church congregation/church organization have a mission statement that expresses an inclusive and queer-friendly welcoming culture? Is this mission statement known to the public? Where can it be found?
- Are the employees of my parish/church organization sensitive to potential negative experiences of non-heterosexual and non-cisgender advice seekers?
- Are the employees of my church congregation/church organization trained with regard to experiences of discrimination and supporting the processes of coming out or transitioning?
- Is everyone in my church congregation/church organization aware that queer pastoral care seekers may have experienced specific social challenges and homo- and/or trans hostile violence?
- Is my parish/church organization connected with LGBTQI+ networks and counseling services etc. and refers to their expertise when needed?

3 Consequences

Queer-affirming chaplains should be aware:
- that the gender identity of those seeking pastoral care is not necessarily female or male. They should display sensitivity to this and, if in doubt, ask which pronouns pastoral care seekers would like to be known by.
- that the sexual orientation of those seeking pastoral care is not necessarily heterosexual. They should display sensitivity to this and avoid making generalized statements.
- of reflecting on their own prejudices and reservations towards queer people and to change them if necessary.
- of working out their own attitude towards queer issues.
- of examining their own behavior and to change it if necessary.
- of acquiring knowledge of queer issues and the challenges faced by queer people.
- of the need to listen, to take their time, to create safe(r) spaces.
- of the need to be empathetic and appreciative.
- to show respect.
- of viewing queer pastoral care seekers as experts in their own stories and to take them seriously.
- of the fact that queer people have experienced minority stress and (spiritual) violence and can be severely traumatized.
- that they should have pastoral care boundaries in mind and refer to professionals, queer-affirming networks, and counseling services as appropriate.

Safe(r) space checklist – "Safe(r) Spaces" in Pastoral Care

"Safe(r) spaces" are rooms and spaces to which people who feel vulnerable or discriminated against can retreat. They are often referred to as "safer" rather than "safe" because absolute safety cannot be guaranteed.

Safer planning spaces
(information and arrangements in advance of pastoral care)
- Information on pastoral confidentiality.
- Inquire about any additional support needs of those seeking pastoral care.
- Agreements on place, time and length of the conversation(s).
- Agreements on content, topics and any specific wishes of those seeking pastoral care.
- Other: _____

Safer meeting spaces
- Queer-friendly welcome signs (e.g. rainbow flags, rainbow posters).
- Queer-friendly social media presence (e.g. #allarewelcome, #queer, #queerfaith).
- Barrier-free and closed rooms.
- No transparent doors.
- Hospitable ambience: Offer coffee, tea, water, cookies and/or fruit if necessary.
- Respect, appreciation and empathy towards those seeking pastoral care.
- Sufficient time and quiet space for conversations.
- Secure environment, in a secured setting, if necessary.
- Other: _____

Safer language
(for one-on-one and group conversations)
- Asking for preferred pronouns for addressing seekers of pastoral care (he, she, they, or no pronoun at all).
- Clear rules of conversation:
  - I-messages
  - Appreciative language
  - Listen and hear out
  - No verbal, nonverbal, or physical assaults
- No derogatory or insulting statements
  - about the skin color of a person

- about the language/accent/dialect of a person
- about the body and body shape of a person
- about the age of a person
- about the gender identity of a person
- about the sexual orientation of a person
- about physical or mental impairments of a person
- about religious beliefs of a person
- Other: _____

A "safe(r) space" is about creating a hospitable and safe environment and treating each other with respect. When a person enters a "safe(r) space", they should be able to feel safe that they will not be discriminated against, insulted or harassed.

Literature

Althaus-Reid, M. (2000): Indecent Theology. Abingdon.
Althaus-Reid, M. (2003): The Queer God. London/New York.
Augsburger, D. W. (1986): Pastoral Counseling Across Cultures. Philadelphia.
Bistum Mainz (2022): "Das schaffen wir nicht alleine". https://bistummainz.de/pressemedien/aktuell/nachrichten/nachricht/Das-schaffen-wir-nicht-alleine/? (access 11.2.2022).
Bolz-Weber, N. (2016): Ich finde Gott in den Dingen, die mich wütend machen. Pastorin der Ausgestoßenen (3. edition). Moers.
Brinkschröder, M. (2006): Sodom als Symptom. Gleichgeschlechtliche Sexualität im christlichen Imaginären – eine religionsgeschichtliche Anamnese. Berlin/New York.
Brinkschröder, M./Ehebrecht-Zumsande, J./Gräwe, V./Mönkebüscher, B./Werner, G. (Ed.) (2022): #OutInChurch. Für eine Kirche ohne Angst. Freiburg i. Br.
Bundesministerium der Justiz (1980): Gesetz über die Änderung der Vornamen und die Feststellung der Geschlechtszugehörigkeit in besonderen Fällen (Transsexuellengesetz – TSG). https://www.gesetze-im-internet.de/tsg/BJNR016540980.html (access 11.2.2022).
Bundesministerium der Justiz (2020): Gesetz zum Schutz vor Konversionsbehandlungen (KonvBG). https://www.gesetze-im-internet.de/konvbehschg/BJNR128500020.html (access 11.2.2022).
Bundesministerium für Familie, Senioren, Frauen und Jugend und Bundesministerium der Justiz (2022): Eckpunkte des Bundesministeriums für Familie, Senioren, Frauen und Jugend und des Bundesministeriums der Justiz zum Selbstbestimmungsgesetz. https://www.bmfsfj.de/resource/blob/199382/1e751a6b7f366eec396d146b3813eed2/20220630-selbstbestimmungsgesetz-eckpunkte-data.pdf (access 11.20.2022).
Cannon, K. (1988): Black Womanist Ethics. Oxford.
Cheng, P. (2011): Radical Love. An Introduction to Queer Theology. New York.
Clifford, J. (2019): The Gospel According to Jesus, Queen of Heaven. London.
Dgti e. V. (Ed.) (2017): Reformation für Alle*. Transidentität/Transsexualität und Kirche. Berlin. https://www.kirchenrecht-ekd.de/document/12484 (access 11.2.2022).
Evangelische Kirche in Deutschland (EKD) (2009): Kirchengesetz zum Schutz des Seelsorgegeheimnisses (Seelsorgegeheimnisgesetz) vom 28.10.2009 (ABl. EKD 2009, p. 352).
Evangelische Kirche in Hessen und Nassau (EKHN) (Ed.) (2018): Zum Bilde Gottes geschaffen. Transsexualität in der Kirche. Wiesbaden.
Gräwe, M./Johannemann, H./Klein, M. (Ed.) (2021): Katholisch und Queer. Eine Einladung zum Hinsehen, Verstehen und Handeln. Paderborn.
Greenough, C. (2020): Queer Theologies. The Basics. London, New York.
Häneke, F. (2019): LGBTIQ* Pfarrer*innen in Deutschland. https://www.feinschwarz.net/lgbtiq-pfarrerinnen-in-deutschland (access 11.2.2022).
Harasta, E. (Ed.) (2016): Traut euch. Schwule und lesbische Ehe in der Kirche. Berlin.
Hartmann, I./Knieling, R. (2016): Gemeinde neu denken. Geistliche Orientierung in wachsender Komplexität (2. edition). Gütersloh.
Heyward, C. (1989): Und sie rührte sein Kleid an. Eine feministische Theologie der Beziehung. Stuttgart.
Hirschberg, C./Freudenberg, M./Plisch, U.-K. (Ed.) (2021): Handbuch Studierendenseelsorge. Gemeinden – Präsenz an der Hochschule – Perspektiven. Göttingen.

Hirschfeld-Eddy-Stiftung (2020): Aufklären, sensibilisieren, vernetzen. LSBTI*-Rechte sind Menschenrechte! Köln/Berlin.
Kremer, R. (2016). Seelsorge im Blaulichtgewitter: Eine pastoraltheologische Untersuchung zur Notfallseelsorge. Stuttgart.
Lesben- und Schwulenverband Deutschland (LSVD) (2021): Homophobe und transfeindliche Gewaltvorfälle in Deutschland (PDF-Brochure): https://www.lsvd.de/de/ct/3958-Alltag-Homophobe-und-transfeindliche-Gewaltvorfaelle-in-Deutschland (access 4.10.2022).
Lesben- und Schwulenverband Deutschland (LSVD) (2022): Soll das Geschlecht jetzt abgeschafft werden? 12 Fragen und Antworten zu Trans* Geschlechtlichkeit (PDF-Broschüre). https://www.lsvd.de/media/doc/6417/2022._soll_geschlecht_jetzt_abgeschafft_werden._broschuere_selbstbestimmungsgesetz.pdf (access 11.2.2022).
Lings, R. (2013): Lost in Translation. Homosexuality in the Bible. Trafford.
Lorde, A. (1984/2021): Sister Outsider. Essays. Berlin.
Lüdtke, K.-P. (2017): Jesus liebt Trans. Transidentität in Familie und Kirchengemeinde. Göppingen.
Meister, G. (2019): Sexualität und Kirche. Gottesdienst- und Andachtspraxis zu Homo-, Bi-, Trans- und Intersexualität. Göttingen.
Meyer, I. H. (1995): Minority Stress and Mental Health in Gay Men. Journal of Health and Social Behavior, 36, pp. 38–56.
Ökumenische Arbeitsgruppe Homosexuelle und Kirche (HuK) e. V. (Ed.) (2018): Verschaffe mir Recht. Kriminalisierung von Lesben, Schwulen, Bisexuellen und Transgendern und die katholische Kirche. München.
Pithan, A./Söderblom, K./Uppenkamp, V. (2019): Leitlinien sexueller Orientierung/Geschlechtsidentitäten. file:///C:/Users/ESG/Downloads/01_Leitlinien-Sexuelle-Orientierung-_15-07-19%20(3).pdf (access 11.24.2022).
Platte, T. (Ed.) (2018): Nicht mehr schweigen. Der lange Weg queerer Christinnen und Christen zu einem authentischen Leben. Berlin.
Plisch, U.-K. (2016): Liebe Deine*n Nächste*n. Gleichgeschlechtliche Liebe und die Bibel. In: Harasta, E. (Ed.): Traut euch. Schwule und lesbische Ehe in der Kirche (pp. 20–36). Berlin.
Plisch, K.-U./Ritter, C. (2022): Lebensentwürfe und Gendergerechtigkeit. In: Hirschberg, C./Freudenberg, M./Plisch, U.-K. (Ed.): Handbuch Studierendenseelsorge. Gemeinden – Präsenz an der Hochschule – Perspektiven (pp. 326–333). Göttingen.
Raastad, H. (2022): This Queer Grace. My lesbian journey through unknown landscapes. A spiritual memoir. Niewegein.
Schinzler, N. (2018): Zur Situation von trans* Kindern und Jugendlichen – insbesondere in Familie und Schule. Bundeszentrale für politische Bildung. Dossier: Geschlechtliche Vielfalt – trans*. https://www.bpb.de/gesellschaft/gender/geschlechtliche-vielfalt-trans/269316/zur-situation-von-trans-kindern-und-jugendlichen (access 11.2.2022).
Schneider, R. (2021): Internalisierte LGBT*-Phobie und LGBT*-Minoritätenstress: die psychischen Folgen der kirchlichen Verurteilung. In: Gräwe, M./Johannemann, H./Klein, M. (Ed.): Katholisch und Queer. Eine Einladung zum Hinsehen, Verstehen und Handeln (pp. 190–200). Paderborn.
Schottroff, L. (1990): Befreiungserfahrungen. Studien zur Sozialgeschichte des Neuen Testaments. München.
Schreiber, G. (Ed.) (2016): Transsexualität in Theologie und Neurowissenschaften. Ergebnisse, Kontroversen, Perspektiven. Berlin/Boston.
Schüssler-Fiorenza, E. (1988): Zu ihrem Gedächtnis. Eine feministisch-theologische Rekonstruktion der christlichen Ursprünge. München/Mainz.
Schulz, E. (2022): Gnade ist immer trotzdem. Als Christin homosexuell? Eine Suche nach Antwort. Neukirchen-Vluyn.
Söderblom, K. (2009): Religionspädagogik der Vielfalt. Herausforderungen jenseits der Hetero-

normativität. In: Pithan, A./Arzt, S./Jakobs, M./Knauth, T. (Ed.): Gender – Religion – Bildung. Beiträge zu einer Religionspädagogik der Vielfalt (pp. 371–386). Gütersloh.
Söderblom, K. (2013): Lebensformen im Pfarrhaus. In: Mantei, S./Sommer, R./Wagner-Rau, U. (Ed.): Geschlechterverhältnisse und Pfarrberuf im Wandel. Irritationen, Analysen und Forschungsperspektiven (pp. 135–146). Stuttgart.
Söderblom, K. (2015): Schulseelsorge für lesbische Mädchen und schwule Jungs als Beitrag für eine Pastoraltheologie der Vielfalt. In: Breckenfelder, M. (Ed.): Homosexualität und Schule (pp. 259–270). Opladen u. a.
Söderblom, K. (2016): Ohne Vorbehalte. https://kerstin-soederblom.de/ohne-vorbehalte/ (access 11.10.2022).
Söderblom, K. (2020a): Queer theologische Notizen. Niewegein.
Söderblom, K. (2020b): Queere Theologie als Dimension einer inklusiven Religionspädagogik der Vielfalt. In: Knauth, T./Möller, R./Pithan, A. (Ed.): Inklusive Religionspädagogik der Vielfalt. Konzeptionelle Grundlagen und didaktische Konzeptionen (pp. 147–157). Münster/New York.
Söderblom, K. (2020c): "Queer und outside the box". https://www.futur2.org/article/queer-und-outside-the-box/ (access 11.2.2022).
Söderblom, K. (2021a): Queere Theologie – Suchbewegungen im Plural. In: V. Dinkelaker, V./Peilstöcker, M. (Ed.): G*tt w/m/d. Geschlechtervielfalt seit biblischen Zeiten (pp. 162–168). Oppenheim am Rhein.
Söderblom, K. (2021b): Versöhnung. Anstoß am Morgen im SWR 1: https://www.kirche-im-swr.de/beitraege/?id=34492 (access 11.2.2022).
Söderblom, K. (2021c): Zachäus und die Scham. https://www.evangelisch.de/blogs/kreuzqueer/181383/20-01-2021 (access 11.2.2022).
Tonstad, L. (2018): Queer Theology. Beyond Apologetics. Eugene.
Vecera, S. (2022): Wie ist Jesus weiß geworden? Mein Traum von einer Kirche ohne Rassismus. Ostfildern.
Verband der Evangelischen Studierendengemeinden in Deutschland (Ed.) (2019): Die Ehe für alle. Eine Handreichung der Bundes-ESG. Hannover.
Weiß, H. (2011): Seelsorge. Supervision. Pastoralpsychologie. Neukirchen-Vluyn.
Wenn Herr Pfarrer zur Pfarrerin wird: Elke kämpft um ihre Gemeinde (2020). Director: M. Rees. Deutschland, Westdeutscher Rundfunk.
Wie Gott uns schuf – Coming-out in der katholischen Kirche (2022). Director: H. Seppelt. Deutschland, Mitteldeutscher Rundfunk.
Wolfrum, S. (2019): Endlich ich. Ein transsexueller Pfarrer auf dem Weg zu sich selbst. München.

Examples of international queer-affirming religious networks

European Forum of LGBTI+ Christian Groups: www.lgbtchristians.eu/
Global Interfaith Network. For People of all Sexes, Sexual Orientations, Gender Identities and Expressions (GIN SSOGIE): https://gin-ssogie.org/
Global Network of Rainbow Catholics: https://rainbowcatholics.org/ ILGA Europe: www.ilga-europe.org/
Metropolitan Community Churches (MCC): https://www.mccchurch.org/landing.html
Rainbow Pilgrims of Faith: https://rainbowpilgrims.faith/
Zwischenraum: https://www.zwischenraum.net/gruppen/

Thank you

When some of my friends from the European Forum of LGBTI+ Christian Groups asked me about my book on queer-affirming pastoral care, I used to apologize that it was written in German. Never in my life would I have thought that a translation into English was a possible option. However, more people from different European countries approached me and urged me to have the book translated. "We don´t have any literature about queer-affirming pastoral care in our country!" many of them stated. "But it is urgently needed!"

After some deliberation with colleagues and friends I felt encouraged to have it translated. Without my friend Max Helmich, translator, teacher and counselor for trans* persons, it would not have been possible. Max translated my book in a surprisingly short amount of time. After that Carol Joyner, my dear sister from the European Forum of LGBTI+ Christian Groups, entered the fray. She volunteered to revise the translation, being herself an author, translator and native speaker. Carol kept the tight time framework and did the work almost immediately after she got the texts.

Without Max and Carol the whole project would not have worked out. Thank you so much to both of you! I also want to thank the colleagues of the Ecumenical Center of the Protestant Church of Hesse and Nassau (EKHN). They were the first to confirm that they would support the project financially. Last but not least, I want to thank all my siblings from the European Forum of LGBTI+ Christian Groups. For more than 25 years, they have been my European family of choice. And the European Forum also supported the publishing of the English edition financially.

The European Forum of LGBTI+ Christian Groups is an ecumenical association of more than 40 queer Christian groups and networks from more than 25 countries in Europe. The European Forum aims to achieve equality and inclusion for LGBTI+ people within and through Christian churches, other religious bodies and multilateral organisations. The European Forum works for freeedom of religions, for human rights and dignity for queer people and for an affirmative discours on human sexuality. The European Forum of LGBTI+ Christian groups enjoys participatory status with the Council of Europe.

For more information please contact members of the board:
www.lgbtchristians.eu